THE PLIGHT OF WESTERN RELIGION

PAUL GIFFORD

The Plight of
Western Religion

The Eclipse of the Other-Worldly

HURST & COMPANY, LONDON

First published in the United Kingdom in 2019 by
C. Hurst & Co. (Publishers) Ltd.,
41 Great Russell Street, London, WC1B 3PL
© Paul Gifford, 2019
All rights reserved.
Printed in the United Kingdom by Bell & Bain Ltd, Glasgow

The right of Paul Gifford to be identified as the author of
this publication is asserted by him in accordance with the
Copyright, Designs and Patents Act, 1988.

A Cataloguing-in-Publication data record for this book
is available from the British Library.

ISBN: 9781787381339 *hardback*

This book is printed using paper from registered sustainable
and managed sources.

www.hurstpublishers.com

CONTENTS

ACKNOWLEDGEMENTS

My greatest indebtedness will become obvious from the endnotes.

There are many others who have in recent years helped me think about religion, among them: Richard Fardon, Eva Spies, Paula Schrode, Brian Dive, Kevin Foley, Graeme Wright, Michael Donnelly, Biruk Tsegaye, Michael Pender, Anthony Chennells, Tim Dyce, Jane Soothill, James Kapalo, Patrick Claffey, Greg Deacon, Emily Welty, Gwen Heaner, Christine Bodewes, Mamadou Diallo, Ibrahima Sow, Bakary Sambe, Harold Miller, Jesse Mugambi, Mark Shaw, Laurenti Magesa, Wanjiru Gitau, Stan Cho Ilo, Silvia Cristofori, Mike Budde, Sean McEntee, Ken Woodward, Kevin Ward, Klaus-Heinrich Hock, John Parker, Christopher Clapham, Richard Bartholomew, Hugh Osgood, Joachim Persoon, Rob James, Jo Sadgrove and Mark Faulkner.

And, as much as any, the late Adrian Hastings, Richard Gray, Carl Fredrik Hallencreutz and John Peel.

Acknowledging their help does not imply that they would agree with all, indeed any, of the views expressed here.

I also thank Francesc Serés and Gavina Freixa of Faber, Arts, Sciences and Humanities Residency of Catalonia, for their faultless academic hospitality.

PREFACE

The origins of this book are largely personal. Since the early 1980s I
have been studying religion in Africa (at the beginning Christianity
exclusively, but in recent years also Islam). My wife has had various
positions across Africa, mainly with the United Nations, and we have
been lucky enough to be based for years at a time in countries as diverse
as Zimbabwe, Ghana, Kenya, Senegal and Ethiopia. I have also spent
shorter periods in other places. At the same time, I have kept one foot
in Europe—since 1992 in the Department for the Study of Religions at
SOAS, a constituent college of the University of London. Since the early
1980s, I have spent almost equal time in Africa and Europe.

These years have witnessed the transformation of Christianity in
Africa. The mainline or mission churches remain powerful (sometimes
the most salient institutions of civil society), the traditional independent churches have lost ground, and newer churches have mush-
roomed. In 2007, when we lived in Kenya where it is required that
churches be registered before operating, the Attorney General
announced that the country had 8,520 registered churches, had 6,740
applications pending, and that 60 new applications were filed every
month. The procedure for vetting new bodies was overwhelmed and
systems had totally broken down.[1] Other African countries have seen
similar proliferation.

My method of study has been empirical. I simply attend as many
churches as I can. In Liberia in 1988–89, beginning at about 6 am and
finishing about 9 pm, I managed to average five churches a Sunday,
mainline, independent and new. (I have not even attempted to keep

PREFACE

that up.) I have supplemented Sunday services by attending Bible studies, crusades and conventions. Media productions have provided supplementary material. All this has taught me the complexity of Christianity in Africa, and the many roles the various forms of Christianity play. Just as importantly, it has disclosed the pervasive 'enchanted religious imagination', or the worldview which seeks causality in spiritual forces.

Not every aspect of Africa's booming Christianity has been uncontroversial. Thus in early 2018 the admittedly hyper-authoritarian President Kagame of Rwanda simply closed 6,000 (yes, six thousand) churches in the country, because if he is to make Rwanda the Singapore of Africa, there are certain kinds of religion that in his opinion Rwanda does not need.[2] The complexity and the controversial nature of some forms of African Christianity have perhaps not received the attention they deserve.

At the same time, teaching in London, I have tried to keep abreast of the situation in the West. I have observed first-hand the declining church attendance, and tried to keep up with literature on the subject. Moreover, I have learnt much from teaching at SOAS. For example, the Religion Department offered introductory courses in many religions, and even when relatively senior I held out to teach the introductory course in Christianity. In that way I could experience secularisation advancing year by year. The students, from many different countries, were intelligent, articulate, extremely knowledgeable about all kinds of things and committed to all sorts of causes, but increasingly less grounded in and drawn to any recognisably Christian heritage.

However, it was not just the declining significance of Christianity that struck me. It was the form of Christianity found in Western churches generally and which characterised even the committed Christians among the students. This was, in most cases, and in striking contrast to the situation in Africa, a completely 'disenchanted' Christianity—one thoroughly in keeping with the surrounding milieu. This increased my reluctance to talk easily of Christianity's shift from the North to the South, for that often implied that what was becoming less significant in the North was the very same animal that was exploding in the South. It wasn't.

I have written elsewhere of what I have learnt of African Christianity. This is my attempt to address what I have observed—often by contrast—of Western Christianity, and to suggest, not least to myself, an explanation not only for Western Christianity's decline, but for the particular disenchanted form in which it has come to be found.

ABBREVIATIONS

BSA	British Sociological Association
CISA	Catholic Information Service for Africa
CUP	Cambridge University Press
EPPC	Ethics and Public Policy Center
Fcfa	Franc of the Communauté financière africaine
IFAN	Institut Fondamental d'Afrique Noire
IMF	International Monetary Fund
IRS	Internal Revenue Service
JCR	*Journal of Contemporary Religion*
LRB	*London Review of Books*
MQUP	McGill-Queen's University Press
NGO	Non-Governmental Organisation
NYRB	*New York Review of Books*
OUP	Oxford University Press
SPCK	Society for Promoting Christian Knowledge
TLS	*Times Literary Supplement*
UCC	United Church of Canada
UNICEF	United Nations Children's Fund
WCC	World Council of Churches

INTRODUCTION

John Peel has remarked, in reference to conversion in Africa:

> The only *workable* definition of conversion is the process by which
> people come to regard themselves, and be regarded by others, as
> Christians. This social identification is what being a Christian most
> immediately and unarguably *is*, rather than holding certain beliefs or
> behaving in certain ways specified a priori ... By taking social identifi-
> cation as the real thing to be explained we avoid the analytical problems
> which arise if—as often occurs in practice—Christians maintain or
> later adopt "non-Christian" beliefs and practices but still insist on
> regarding themselves as Christians and are so regarded by others.[1]

So, for Peel, social identification is what being a Christian *is*; digging
deeper or pushing further leads to 'unworkable' analytical problems.
Certainly, there is much that can be discussed under the heading of
social identification, as Peel ably shows in his justly acclaimed study.
However, in this book I want go beyond labelling to address some of
the analytical problems he sidesteps or leaves aside, especially the 'certain beliefs ... specified a priori'.

I attempt this through an analysis of Western Christianity over
recent centuries. For this exercise I adopt a substantive definition of
religion (activity premised on the existence of superhuman powers)
because it enables me to attempt to differentiate religion from culture, ethnicity, politics and morality. I argue that religion, understood
substantively, necessarily implies a perception of reality, and in the
West until recent centuries (as in so many cultures still) the ordinary,
natural and immediate way of experiencing and understanding reality

has been in terms of otherworldly or spiritual forces. However, a cognitive shift has taken place through the rise of science and its subsequent technological application. This new consciousness has not disproved the existence of spiritual forces, but it has led to the peripheralisation of the otherworldly, which mainline Western churches seem to accept; they persist, often as significant players in society, but increasingly as pressure groups promoting 'humanist' values and as agencies effecting them. Claims of 'American exceptionalism'—that Americans' constant invocation of Christianity shows that, in contrast to Europeans, Americans have retained an awareness of the supernatural—are misleading; phenomena like Evangelical support for President Trump, and the mega-church message of success in the capitalist system, can be understood as political and cultural rather than religious. This peripheralising of the otherworldly constitutes a watershed in human history, with profound consequences not just for religious institutions but for our entire world order.

I make my argument in five chapters. Chapter 1 identifies many of the issues under discussion. I try to bring some clarity into contemporary debate on religion, particularly by differentiating issues of culture, identity and tradition in any such discussion. I also defend my focus on 'belief' or the cognitive element in religion. Chapter 2 attempts to trace the cognitive shift that has taken place in the West in recent centuries, and to illustrate this shift through a comparison with an example of non-Western religion. Chapter 3 addresses some counterclaims, for example that the 'New Age' or counterculture shows that religion is alive and well in the West, just 'mutating' or becoming personalised. I illustrate the decline of Christianity in Victorian times and in the 1960s, and show how 'internally secularised' or hollowed out many contemporary forms of Western Christianity have become. Chapter 4 illustrates the hollowness of claims of 'American exceptionalism'. Chapter 5 pulls the argument together, arguing that a *rationality of functional instrumentality* (explained below) has become the dominant cognitive style in all modern societies, a cognitive style which strongly militates against a substantively religious understanding of reality.

1

ISSUES

Religion: clarifying the idea

In debates about religion, it is helpful to be clear about exactly what is under discussion. Berger has claimed: 'I once asked Luckmann who would *not* be religious by his definition. He replied, "A dog."'[1] But if everything or anything or anyone is by definition religious, it is hard to use the term analytically. It is impossible to compare and contrast with anything else (because there is nothing else). It is impossible to differentiate religion from something like culture or ethnicity, which is precisely what I attempt here. So in what follows, I will adopt a substantive definition like Reisebrodt's: 'Religion is a complex of practices based on the premise of the existence of superhuman powers'.[2] There is nothing remarkable in this- -it is a definition of fine pedigree, adopted by prominent scholars of religion like Taylor, Bruce, Martin and Berger.[3]

I am aware of the debates about substantive versus functional definitions (religion in a functional sense is anything addressing deeper questions or needs or values). I have no need to consider those here.[4] I adopt a substantive definition because it enables me to draw attention to some changes in Western societies about which confusion often reigns, and because it enables me to pinpoint significant differences between the West and many other cultures. I adopt a substantive definition because it serves my present purpose.[5]

Some are reluctant to define religion in this way. For Luckmann, as noted above, everything and everyone is religious. Comte and Bakunin spoke of a religion of humanity. Dworkin proposes a 'religion without God' and takes two values, 'life's intrinsic meaning and nature's intrinsic beauty', as 'paradigms of a full religious attitude to life'.[6] Beckford defined religion as 'concern for the "felt whole" or for the ultimate significance of things'.[7] In a later work, he let religion mean whatever people mean when they use the term.[8] So, too, Malory Nye.[9] For Herberg, 'one's ultimate, over-all way of life is one's religion'.[10] For Hervieu-Léger, religion is a 'chain of memory' bringing individuals into a collectivity.[11] Matthew Arnold defined religion as 'that which binds and holds us to the practice of righteousness'.[12] Eagleton writes of religion in terms of its functions; where such functions are met (as, in his opinion, in sport) you seemingly have religion.[13] All these authors have much to contribute (and, in the case of Eagleton, plenty of knockabout entertainment as well). I am not necessarily attempting to refute any of them; I am simply doing something different.

Heelas and Woodhead deliberately seek to avoid a narrow definition: 'One of our aims ... is to get away from monolithic understandings of religion'.[14] McLeod claims the secularisation thesis depends on a 'too narrow' understanding (the understanding adopted here).[15] Of course, all admit that in legal contexts, for example, precision is necessary: thus Scientology meets the legal definition required in Britain and Australia; it does not in Austria and Belgium. But defining religion substantively can bring clarity to discussions where imprecision is all too common. Was America's civil rights movement secular or religious? In his study of American religion from Eisenhower to Obama, Woodward, *Newsweek*'s religious correspondent for nearly forty years, answers clearly: 'At *Newsweek* ... the civil rights movement was seen as essentially secular, with black churches serving as its institutional staging ground of convenience.'[16] By contrast, a study by Douthat of the *New York Times* covering roughly the same ground can readily talk of 'the Christian character of the civil rights movement', and even suggest that only when it can find a similar cause will American Christianity regain its former vitality.[17] Since neither Woodward nor Douthat bothers to tell us what they mean by religion, it is difficult to take sides in such a debate.

Defining religion substantively also enables me to avoid some mine-fields. Thus MacCulloch: '"Religion" is a concept imposed on human behaviour by one variant of Christianity, post-Reformation Protestantism. Most people in the history of the human race would be hard put to separate out a "religious" element from the range of things they do to survive and build up a sense of themselves and the world around them.'[18] True, until exposed to modern Western culture, most would have been unable to identify a 'religious' dimension; it was simply life as it was lived. Peel has observed that the Yoruba expressed it in the pidgin phrase 'making country fashion'; their religion was simply what the Yoruba did, as the English colonists did Anglicanism and the French did Catholicism. But the Yoruba cosmology with their array of gods was real, long before any post-Reformation imposition. Likewise Jonathan Smith: 'Religion is solely the creation of the scholar's study. It is created for the scholar's analytic purposes ... Religion has no independent existence apart from the academy.'[19] Yet the Yoruba otherworldly cosmology was there long before any scholar addressed it. It was simply so woven into everything else there was no need to isolate it—or, indeed, any ability to do so. Cavanaugh can claim that 'there is no such thing as a transhistorical or transcultural "religion" that is essentially separate from politics'.[20] But there is; a worldview based on spiritual causality is identifiable enough and can be distinguished from one that is not, and the political ramifications of this dimension are a distinct and subsequent issue. Religion as discussed in this book is not purely a reconstruction on our part.

Current discussion of religion frequently uses the words 'spirituality' and 'religiosity' and 'religiousness'. Sometimes these are clarified, but in many cases they serve, intentionally or not, further to confuse what is being discussed. In what follows, if 'spirituality' and 'religiousness' genuinely involve some relation to otherworldly forces, we have religion in the sense understood in this book. Commenting on a Pew Report, the religious correspondent of *The Economist* gave a shorthand description of those declaring themselves 'spiritual': they are 'those who rarely if ever attend an act of worship but seem sensitive to their human and physical environment and exude a sort of connection with the world'. Human or ecological sensitivity and connectedness do not constitute religion in the sense under discussion here, nor do 'implicit

religion', 'civil religion', 'secular religion' unless they have some reference to a reality of another order.[21]

Understanding religion in a substantive way enables me to differentiate it from other dimensions, cultural or political or economic; not
invariably or perfectly, of course, but in some cases adequately and
significantly. A certain lack of clarity can arise when religion is invoked
too readily. The novelist Zadie Smith in an address accepting a literature prize stated (in making the point that homogeneous societies are
not exempt from some of the problems of heterogeneous societies):
'Northern Ireland, an area where people who look absolutely identical
to each other, eat the same food, pray to the same God, read the same
holy book, wear the same clothes, and celebrate the same holidays have
yet spent four hundred years at war over a relatively minor doctrinal
difference they later allowed to morph into an all-encompassing argument over land, government, and national identity.'[22] It may seem
ungenerous to challenge a throwaway illustration in a stimulating
address, but singling out 'a minor doctrinal difference' as the cause of
'the Troubles' in Northern Ireland is profoundly tendentious. If one
wants to single out one cause, far more important is surely the fact that
a plantation of immigrants dispossessed the indigenes. Yes, the immigrants were identified with a different form of Christianity from that
of the indigenes, and this difference has undoubtedly at times been
played up as a marker of identity. But to claim religion is the basis of
the Troubles is misleading.

Exactly the same might be said of the Rohingya refugees crossing
from Myanmar into Bangladesh, an international crisis in 2017. Almost
invariably, news reports referred to these refugees as 'Rohingya
Muslims'. Yes, the Rohingya identify overwhelmingly as Muslim, and
some Burmese Buddhist institutions have notoriously initiated a crusade against them, but to fasten on this religious element as their defining characteristic is tendentious (and perhaps not unrelated to the
proliferating bodies committed to monitor 'religious freedom').[23] Such
examples abound. In the clashes in Nigeria's Middle Belt in the last few
decades, the pastoralists certainly identify as Muslim, the settled inhab-
itants as Christian, but surely pastoralists versus farmers would provide
a better analytical starting point than presenting the tension as something *religious* between Muslim and Christian.

Richard Dawkins pushes the privileging of the religious element to its limit. Convinced that religion underlies all conflicts, he writes: 'It is a spade we have here, let's *call* it a spade ... It is time to stop the mealy-mouthed euphemisms: "Nationalists", "Loyalists", "Communities", "Ethnic Groups", "Cultures", "Civilizations". *Religions* is the word you need.'[24] No, it is important to be clear what factors are at play and to what degree, and at least in some cases the religious element can be differentiated from elements like ethnicity and culture and, when so demarcated, can be more accurately assessed regarding importance.

It may well be true that for most of history it was not possible to make such a distinction. Some insist that the Thirty Years War (1618–48) was a war of religion—such as recently the philosopher A.C. Grayling, known for his crusade against religion of all kinds.[25] However, in *The Myth of Religious Violence*, Cavanaugh has well shown that isolating religion as a cause at that time is simply anachronistic. Differentiating religion within a social, political, economic and cultural *Totalität* becomes a possibility only with the rise of the modern world. The Thirty Years War could not be a war of religion, argues Cavanaugh, because religion could not be differentiated then.[26] We have already mentioned Northern Ireland's Troubles. Dawkins is one who claims they were simply 'religious'. Certainly the struggle was between overwhelmingly Protestant Unionists and overwhelmingly Catholic Nationalists, but David Martin maintains that Dawkins has simply failed to differentiate between elements of identity that would need to be differentiated before such a claim could be made.[27] So one might argue that it is incorrect to call either the Northern Ireland conflict or the Thirty Years War 'religious', but for diametrically opposed reasons. It is misleading to label the Thirty Years War religious because religion could not be analytically differentiated then; it is just as misleading to call the Troubles in Northern Ireland religious because when all necessary differentiations are made, religion is not found to be particularly significant.[28]

Differentiation can be pushed even further. It has been claimed that 'by the early eighteenth century, the [Catholic] Church may well have possessed one-sixteenth of the land in Bohemia, two-thirds in the Kingdom of Naples, about one-third in Lombardy, almost a half of the Papal States, perhaps just over a tenth of France, approaching two-fifths of Austria and nearly half of Bavaria'.[29] Possessing such property automatically made the Catholic Church a major player in society, economics and politics. Yet, here we are dealing with an institution functioning in the secular realm, on all fours with other powerful landlords. This phenomenon is evident today. We have raised the question of the religious element in Northern Ireland's Troubles. Fulton has argued that religion did indeed play a considerable part in them, not least because the Catholic Church in the Republic of Ireland sought to maintain its control of education, health and other sectors where it enjoyed a privileged position, and that this pursuit of power and control ('monopoly Catholicism') was a key element in reinforcing the simultaneously defensive and aggressive identity of the Unionists. In this way religious institutions can enter the fray but as *institutions* rather than anything substantively religious.[30] We will return to this.

This is not primarily a sociological study, a study of societies and the role of religion within them. It is a study of change in the nature of perception. It is tangentially related to the secularisation thesis. In brief, the secularisation thesis is a loose collection of ideas that claim that with modernity, religion loses its salience because of differentiation, societalisation (the move from rural to urban), and rationalisation. Bruce expresses it alliteratively: it is a set of associated ideas about the decline in the modern world of the prestige, power, popularity, plausibility and presence of religion.[31] To give some idea of what the secularisation thesis refers to, and the increasing momentum of the process in recent decades, consider the following (I will not give references; such data are continually published; these are simply some among the many I have collected in recent years). In Britain in 2016, the proportion of those saying that they had no religion (49% in the 2015 data) overtook those saying they were Christian (43% in 2015). In England in 1957, 55% said they belonged to the Church of England, in 1983 the figure was 40%, and in 2017 the number was 15% (with a mere 3% in the 18–24 age bracket, in contrast to 40% of those aged over 75). Britain's United Reformed Church dropped 43% in attendance between 1998 and 2005. Britain's Methodist Church had 330,000 members in 2005, compared with a million a generation previously (and in the three years before 2005 it had seen a 30% drop in numbers of children and young people).[32]

Similar trends are found elsewhere. In France, weekly mass attendance dropped from 20% in 1972 to 4.5% in 2009. In Spain in 2004, only 18% declared themselves to be practising Catholics, compared with 98% fifty years before. In Canada, Catholic weekly mass attendance in 1957 was 88% in Quebec and 75% outside Quebec province; by 2000 the figures were 23% for Quebec and 29% outside. In September 2017, 27% of Americans reported thinking of themselves as 'spiritual but not religious', up 8 percentage points in five years.

In what follows I will not be continually rehearsing such statistics (and I will shortly highlight some of the limitations in establishing them). It is the explanation of such statistics that is my concern, if in an unconventional way. As I will have frequent occasion to remark, it is widely accepted that the secularisation thesis is discredited. I will argue that this view is erroneous, and arises from confusion over what is being discussed. Berger's famous recantation of the secularisation thesis (where necessary below, I will use the terms Younger Berger and Older Berger to differentiate) is based on such confusion. Throughout his life, in both earlier and later writings, he insists on a substantive definition.[33] Yet he gives three reasons for his recantation: the resurgence of religion in the third world; the counterculture; the Evangelical revival.[34] We can leave aside the third world; the fact that virtually everyone in Niger is religious has simply no relevance for the secularisation thesis. And since the population of Niger and similar countries is growing exponentially (in Niger in 2017 women averaged 6.7 children), of course the number of religious people in the world is higher than ever. That is also of no relevance for the secularisation thesis. But as regards his second and third reasons, the extent to which the counterculture and American Evangelicalism are substantively religious would need to be demonstrated, not presumed. Berger has not even attempted to demonstrate that America's counterculture and Evangelical revival meet his substantive criteria for religion. His recantation involves quietly sliding from a substantive definition of religion to something far looser. The same slippage, I will show, is found in scholars as diverse as Bruce and Riesebrodt.

Meaning of words

Even self-identification as Christian is not as 'workable' as Peel implies in the quotation in the Introduction above. Richard Hoggart, writing in 1957, said that for his working-class folk, being Christian meant being good, decent and kind, and helping one's neighbour. 'Doing your best to be an "ordinary decent" person—that is what Christianity means really.'[35] Similar conceptions persist in Trump's America; in 2017 *The Economist*, asking why 'Christians can love a much-married braggart', states that for many whites, especially in small towns and rural areas, 'adhering to traditional Bible values and embracing a personal relationship with Jesus Christ—to use one common definition of evangelical faith—is another way of saying "I am an upstanding citizen"'.[36] Claiming to be a Christian need mean little more than that.

Despite the stridency of the New Atheists, Christianity still has positive connotations in much of the world, where it still carries overtones of honesty, justice, fairness and decency. In the jargon of older Oxford philosophy, it is a 'stand up and cheer word' as opposed to a 'go for your gun word'. A recent study examines political leaders for their expressions of notions of God, faith, religion, but it is nowhere made clear how one might assess this. Why would a politician, seeking votes, not stress his or her Christian credentials? It is unlikely to do harm. Conversely, in most Western countries there would be little advantage in downplaying one's Christianity, even less in admitting atheism. Politics is about pursuing policies (often controversial policies like liberal economics, nuclear energy, minority rights) and securing an immediate sympathetic response is crucial. But it cannot be concluded from a politician's referring to God or 'Christian values' that there is any personal commitment to Christianity in any significant sense, or indeed in any sense at all. In that volume, the essay on David Cameron, former Prime Minister of Britain, quotes him saying: 'I am a committed—but, I have to say, vaguely practising—Church of England Christian'.[37] Of itself, such a claim may have very little content. The authors of these essays are perfectly aware of this. Almost every essay stresses it; many chapters specifically allow for the instrumentalisation of Christianity. The chapter on Hungary's Victor Orbán clearly distinguishes his political and cultural 'rather than religious' use of Christianity, and admits that his 'Christian nationalism' could be pure politics.[38] The fact that religion is so politicised in America has to be borne in mind when considering the Christian professions of Presidents like Reagan and Obama, especially when both attended church services so rarely. The chapter on George W. Bush remarks: 'His faith language is, in part at least, simply the language required of the President of the United States.'[39] Such admissions make the overall confusion of Spencer's conclusion even more evident: 'The presence and prevalence of Christian leaders, not least in some of the world's most secular, plural and "modern" countries, remains noteworthy. The idea that "secularization" would purge politics of religious commitment is surely misguided.'[40]

If religion is still widely presumed to make children respectful, adolescents restrained, tradesmen hard-working and bankers honest, most would have little problem in asserting that religion is good for people—if not for themselves, certainly for others. Thus Alastair Campbell, Tony Blair's head of communications, on the promotional blurb for the collection of essays just cited, can state he is a 'pro-faith atheist'. Why wouldn't he be? The churches' social work alone saves the state millions. The poet and critic Clive James, another self-confessed atheist, can insist on preserving the legacy of Jesus: 'the essence of his personality still deserves to be cherished as a salvation, a redemption'.[41] The *Times* columnist Matthew Parris, in a rather controversial column at Christmas 2008 titled 'As an Atheist, I Truly Believe Africa Needs God', advocated sending missionaries rather than aid money (to counter what he called Africa's 'crushing passivity').[42] Their positions are perfectly defensible.

Belief

Peel mentions 'beliefs' as an issue he is reluctant to tackle. Admittedly, the issue is complex. One of the objections to a substantive definition of religion is that it prioritises belief, which (it is alleged) is too bound up with Western Christianity to be taken as constitutive of other religions. Since, of set purpose, I am addressing Western Christianity, this objection is hardly relevant, but raising it does allow me to emphasise that religion substantively understood necessarily implies a cognitive element. Whatever else it may be, a religion comprises an understanding of reality, a worldview, an *imaginaire*, a *Vorstellung*. Many study religion focusing on ritual; much light can be shed thereby, but no ritual will last long if the rationale behind it is no longer persuasive.

Similarly, others study religions focusing on their ethics or morals or in many cases laws, but, again, no practices can long persist if the rationale underpinning them loses its hold. In the words of the Younger Berger: 'It is all very well to say that Judaism is, above all, a matter of practice. This practice is, however, rooted in a specific cognitive universe without which it is threatened with meaninglessness. The numerous pre- and proscriptions of orthodox Judaism are likely to appear as so many absurdities, unless they remain linked to a worldview that includes the supernatural.'[43]

Belief may not always be the right word to convey this cognitive element. If everyone in a culture shares a particular worldview, it is not a belief but *reality*; it is simply the way the world is.[44] As remarked above, most African languages had no word for religion, but that is because the pervasive *imaginaire* was simply taken for granted.

In this book I set out to tackle this matter of belief. This is not easy. The secularisation debate is normally conducted in terms of affiliation, attendance and belief, but it is the belief element that is the least adequately treated. In the British Household Panel survey, for example, there is one question: 'How much difference would you say religious beliefs make to your life?'—allowing for 'a great difference', 'some difference', 'a little' or 'no difference'. The British Social Attitudes survey asks respondents which of six statements 'comes closest to expressing what you believe about God', with the range extending from the definite 'I don't believe in God' to the equally categorical 'I know God really exists and I have no doubts about it'. The Pew Research Centre draws its conclusions on the similarly graded answers to the question 'How important is religion in your life?' WIN-Gallup International drew up a 'Religion and Atheism Index' of 57 countries from answers to the question 'Irrespective of whether you attend a place of worship or not, would you say you are a religious person, not a religious person or a convinced atheist?'[45] There is no need to list similar polls. Even the perfect answers to these four enquiries give little help in establishing definite beliefs, much less in establishing some recognisable form of Christianity.

It is often not clear what it means to believe. One might posit some need to articulate or even defend a belief. The *Times* columnist David Aaronovitch has well described growing up as the son of two of

Britain's prominent members of the Communist Party. He frequently makes the analogy: it was like growing up a Catholic. But this misses one profound difference. His parents in their street preaching had to defend, say, the show trials of Stalin and the invasions of Hungary or Czechoslovakia against a very hostile public. A Catholic's professed belief in the Immaculate Conception of Mary could remain mostly unarticulated and never challenged or even adverted to. The Catholics to whom Aaronovitch compares himself were seldom challenged in daily life to defend their purported beliefs, which could gradually atrophy, at most trotted out on special occasions as a 'formulaic' or 'formalised' doctrine (one affirmed-for-purposes-of-identity-but-in-no-way-significant).[46]

A commonsense interpretation would require some impact on one's life or behaviour. If one leaves substantial money to pay for masses after death, it would on the face of it indicate that one does believe in an afterlife—if one is prepared to hand over one's estate for one's belief, that seems a fairly logical conclusion. Courts in America have in recent years convicted unswerving adherents of the faith gospel (in an extreme form, the belief that God will heal sickness and that recourse to medicine displays a sinful lack of faith) for letting their children die rather than take them to doctors. In such cases beliefs have prima facie had an impact upon conduct.

America has a long history of millenarianism. The Scofield Reference Bible, an edition of the King James Version arranged and annotated according to the pre-millennial dispensationalism of John Nelson Darby, has been for many the Bible of choice; many had no idea that there was any other way of reading the Bible. There are today prominent millennialist preachers who are prepared to describe in graphic detail the imminent end of the world—preachers like Jack Van Impe, John Hagee and most notably Hal Lindsey, whose *Late Great Planet Earth* was in the 1970s and 1980s, according to some estimates, America's bestselling non-fiction book (if such it can be called).[47] Between 1995 and 2007 Tim LaHaye and Jerry Jenkins produced 16 novels in their Left Behind series which sold 60 million copies. The books were premised on the apocalyptic tribulations of the end times and the imminent rapture of believers. Yet readers could apparently be thoroughly gripped by these books without taking any of the steps that would seem required if they believed in any hard sense that the end was imminent. Exactly the same could be said of the apocalyptic strain in the so-called Islamic State. ISIS made great claims for Dabiq, a small town in northern Syria, where according to one hadith the apocalyptic showdown would occur between the faithful of the Caliphate and crusaders from the West. In fact, as opposing forces moved in in late 2016, ISIS troops slunk away with barely a whimper, which on the face of it called into doubt their professed belief in the climactic battle of their apocalyptic theology.

Years ago, Bryan Wilson used the term 'internally secularised' to characterise Christianity in America. Christianity is invoked incessantly, but, no less than in other technologically advanced countries, 'for every social problem, whether of economy, polity, law, education, family relations or recreation, the solutions proposed are not only non-religious, but solutions that depend on technical expertise and bureaucratic organization. Planning, not revelation; rational order, not inspiration; systematic routine, not charismatic or traditional action, are the imperatives in ever widening arenas of public life.'[48] Even for those insisting on creationism, Wilson remarks: 'This pious biblicism appears to have no impact whatsoever on the assumptions on which the social system operates.'[49] This notion of 'internal secularisation' or hollowing out, though sometimes dismissed,[50] is crucial to so much of what follows.

The question of belief needs to be addressed, because this is pre-eminently the area where unfounded assertions abound. Above I mentioned Hoggart's contention that the label Christian meant being kind and decent. He maintains: 'Working-class people, when they insist on a church wedding or funeral, are drawing on beliefs which, though rarely considered, are still in most cases firmly there. These beliefs, some of the basic Christian doctrines, they hold but do not examine.'[51] He gives no idea what basic Christian doctrines they hold, nor in what way.[52] A modern study of the changing face of Irish Catholicism makes a similar claim: 'While levels of orthodox Christian belief remain, religious practice … is declining.'[53] There is no attempt in that article to explain what 'orthodox Christian belief' means (whether the Trinity, the Incarnation, bodily resurrection and so on), nor any indication of how one might establish it, much less assess what significance the professed belief might have. As we shall frequently note, 'believe' in studies of modern religion is often an intransitive verb; people are simply said to believe, or have 'beliefs', but for any intelligent assessment it is often necessary to focus on the transitive element, or give some content to what is believed. That is what is attempted in this book.

The complexity is obvious. Statements about belief may in fact be playing another role altogether. The Trinity is commonly assumed to be the basic doctrine of Christianity. It is central to Muslim anti-Christian polemic, and the first article of the constitution of the World Council of Churches requires for membership a church's expressed belief in the Trinity (along with belief in the divinity of Christ). Yet the Anglican theologian Leslie Houlden can casually write:

> It is hard to see why the classical formulations should constitute a base line for all later reflection ... It is hard to see why "the" (or "a") "doctrine of the Trinity" should be a permanent part of living Christianity. Indeed, outside some styles of technical systematic theology and the official (but fossilized?) formularies, it probably is so no more, for bad reasons as well as good.[54]

If it is indeed the case that the Trinity is no longer part of 'living Christianity', what is *in reality* going on when belief in the Trinity is said to be so essential?

It is in this context that polling must be mentioned. As suggested above, in matters of belief polls are of limited use. In matters of religion, inquiries relate so often to what pollsters call 'motherhood issues' or issues that for the respondents are already loaded. Thus, asked about belief in God or reading the Bible, most Christians know that they are supposed to be in favour of them—or at least this was the case until very recently when in Britain perhaps the default position changed.[55] Similarly, asked if they attend church, Americans give a response that is quite inflated—perhaps by a factor of two, as Hadaway and collaborators established in 1993 (it is the inflated figures that have so often been used to rebut the secularisation thesis).[56] Voas has pointed up the problem clearly:

> Studies on polling show that people are prepared to express opinions about almost anything, whether or not they have any knowledge of or interest in the topic. Such "beliefs" may be uninformed, held superficially, seldom acted upon, and relatively volatile ... We cannot conclude from the fact that people tell pollsters they believe in God that they give the matter any thought, find it significant, will feel the same next year, or plan to do anything about it.[57]

It is often the way the question is framed that opens the door to distortion. Bruce notes of a questionnaire of Ronald Inglehart:

> Inglehart's questionnaire asks: "How often, if at all, do you think about the meaning and purpose of life?" The answer "Never" could be interpreted by respondents as shorthand for "I never think about the meaning and purpose of life because I am crass". Some macho working-class lad might feel obliged to assert "never" in case anyone thought he was an art-lover, but I suspect many people will claim some interest in the meaning of life, just because the opposite could be seen as insulting.[58]

Rodney Stark's *What Americans* Really *Believe*, purporting to establish beyond doubt (and against his understandably numerous critics) America's flourishing Christianity, furnishes several such examples. The responses to an invitation to comment whether 'My life has real purpose' convey little; who wants to condemn him- or herself as a rootless drifter? When asked to comment on 'I am a religious person', who wouldn't answer affirmatively, if the negative is thought to imply that one is a complete materialist or hedonist? Similarly, asked whether one belongs to an organisation, what answer is there if one wants to avoid giving the impression of being in some way antisocial?[59]

Above all, pollsters tend to take the word of interviewees; if they identify themselves as Lutheran or Catholic, this is taken as significant. There is often little attempt to assess what this means, if anything. Often it means no more than that the interviewee was brought up in that tradition, in an age when being brought up in a tradition was the norm; he or she may long have abandoned any meaningful adherence to the beliefs or practices for which the denomination officially stands, yet is far from antagonistic and feels no need positively to repudiate this tradition.

There is the further issue that even when it is established that, say, '81% of white Evangelicals voted for Trump', it is far from clear that being 'Evangelical' is the (or even 'a') significant explanatory factor. 'Southern' or 'rural' or even 'racist' may be far more significant. The key factors may be occupation, level of education, or feeling of alienation. Some scholars, particularly scholars of religion, tend to see religion in play where this would need to be established.

In what follows I will cite statistics occasionally, but with profound reservations stemming from the remarks above. When a 2000 *Newsweek* poll claimed that 77% of Catholics believed in the literal truth of the Bible, obviously some reserve is called for.[60]

Culture

Malory Nye in his introductory *Religion: The Basics*, claims (in a discussion of Weber): 'it is nearly impossible to say where the distinction lies between religion and economics, politics or culture ... The problem ... often comes when we try to isolate "religion" off too much from other cultural activities.'[61] But in this book I argue that in the West today one can attempt exactly this—the differentiation of religion from culture generally. Of course in the past nearly all (all without exception?) cultures have been religious, because for most of human history superhuman forces have played a large part in explaining the world. So too most cultures today. The Older Berger writes: 'In most of the world culture is inextricably linked to religion.'[62] Exactly. However, Berger's qualification ('in most of the world') seems to allow for precisely the point I want to make here: that in contemporary Western societies, this symbiotic union can no longer be presumed.

To appreciate this, consider Christmas. This festival remains one of the fixed points of the calendar in virtually all Western societies. In one sense, of course, it is a Christian feast—it is obviously not Buddhist or Muslim, and it has its origins in the foundational Christian notion of the incarnation of God made man. But it has arguably floated so free of its Christian roots that to invoke the religious element today may obscure rather than elucidate the contemporary reality. It is precisely this religious element that has receded, and in the West religion no longer need form an integral part of culture.

Similarly with the festivals in honour of local saints celebrated all over Catholic Europe. These feasts had their origins in a lively understanding of saints as mediators, intercessors, advocates before God. Devotion to them was one of the principal ways of ensuring salvation—as well, of course, of ensuring protection here below. Today, these festivals are as likely to be promoted by civic authorities or tourist boards, primarily as exhibitions of civic pride and commercial opportunity. There is no reason, of course, why one should not participate in such festivals for spiritual blessings, even to ensure one's eternal

17

salvation, but for most participants today one must query the sense in which these cultural events can be understood as religious.

Such considerations arise with pilgrimages like that to Santiago de Compostela, which in Late Antiquity and the Middle Ages were means of expiating sins, gaining merit and indulgences, remitting temporal punishment, all intimately connected with salvation in the hereafter. There exists a twelfth-century *Guide for Pilgrims to Santiago* which, besides having the distinction of being the earliest extant travellers' guide, illustrates just how supernatural the enterprise was, with book two enumerating the miracles of St James.[63] Of course, there is no reason to ignore the this-worldly function of such pilgrimages, in the case of Compostela most obviously solidarity in the face of the Muslim threat.[64] This Compostela pilgrimage had largely fallen into abeyance, until revived by the tourist boards of Galicia, Asturias, Cantabria and the Basque territories. Since the 1980s it has drawn 'pilgrims' by the hundreds of thousands, avowed agnostics and atheists as much as believers, intent on discovering or refocusing or reorienting them-selves, or just toning up physically. Jean-Christophe Rufin, an avowed atheist, member of the French Academy and co-founder of Médecins Sans Frontières, provides an eloquent example. The conclusion to his quite profound reflections on his own experience and that of his fellow 'pilgrims' is that the pilgrimage to Compostela is not Christian at all; if 'religious' in any sense, it is Buddhist.[65] Perhaps the apogee (or nadir, according to taste) is Shirley MacLaine's pilgrimage, accompanied by a spirit guide Ariel, the soulmate of Michelangelo, a pilgrimage on which she remembered her previous androgenous incarnation in Atlantis and her earlier life as a medieval Moorish princess and Charlemagne's mis-tress.[66] The fact that the tourist industry has twinned this pilgrimage to Compostela with the Shinto–Buddhist pilgrimage of Kumano Kodo in Japan is evidence enough of its dissociation from any specifically Catholic rationale. Failure to attempt to differentiate the religious from other factors can distort the reality. Today, a more revealing approach might be to focus on the specifically non-religious.[67]

This book refers repeatedly to contemporary Western culture. Any talk of Western culture today can be fraught and lead to accusations of Eurocentrism. The claim that such and such is one's culture is often intended to foreclose all debate. Thus President Xi could say to the

ISSUES

United Nations General Assembly in New York in September 2015: 'No civilization is superior to others. Each civilization represents the unique vision and contribution of its people.'[68] As I will argue below, the world has changed in recent centuries; a productive culture has come to dominate the globe, a culture where the place of religion has been radically refashioned. Debates about culture, though enormously fraught, are unavoidable in contemporary discussion of religion.

Identity

In his memoirs, Bernard Lewis, the distinguished historian of the Middle East, recounts an anecdote which well illustrates the complexity of religious identity. In the Second World War, Lewis was in Britain's intelligence corps, intercepting and decoding enemy messages, and two of their number used to be on duty every night in case of emergency. Conversation was often fairly superficial, limited by the 'need to know', but one night his companion began a conversation: 'Forgive me, I don't want to intrude, but am I right in thinking that you are Jewish?' 'You are right. I am Jewish, and there is nothing to forgive.' 'Forgive me, but I have the impression that you are not a devout and observant Jew.' 'You are right again.' Then Lewis's companion admitted he was mystified: why would one be ready to face persecution or death for a religion in which one didn't believe and which one didn't practise?

This led Lewis to explain both to his companion and to himself that Jewishness is a shared memory and experience of life, a many-faceted culture, an identity ('not a whole or exclusive identity, but an important part of the multiple identities that all civilized people bear') and 'a heritage, preserved through millennia by courage, achievement and loyalty, and for all these reasons, a source of legitimate pride to be cherished and passed on to those who come after us'.[69] Lewis has here well expressed the centrality of ethnicity to Jewish identity—even to the extent that any substantive understanding of Judaism may become effectively eclipsed. In what follows, I will be asking how a modern Western Christian might answer the same question, since ethnicity is not a factor in the above sense (though Christianity has assumed considerable ethnic significance in places like Ireland and Poland). I will argue that one may profoundly appreciate one's religious heritage, without in any way feeling the need to identify with the tradition today.

19

The need to identify more precisely the role of religion in identity is becoming salient in an important new form. Just after the election of President Trump, *The Economist* ran a cover story deploring 'The New Nationalism'. The leading editorial stated:

> In Russia Vladimir Putin has shunned cosmopolitan liberal values for a distinctly Russian mix of Slavic tradition and Orthodox Christianity. In Turkey Recep Tayyip Erdogan has turned away from the European Union and from peace talks with the Kurdish minority, in favour of a strident, Islamic nationalism that is quick to detect insults and threats from abroad. In India, Narendra Modi remains outward-looking and modernizing, but he has ties to radical ethnic nationalist Hindu groups that preach chauvinism and intolerance.'[70]

In three sentences, three different religions, Christianity, Islam, Hinduism, are implicated in three diverse 'new nationalisms'. Surely that is too glib. In all three cases the reality is that many people, unhappy with contemporary trends that they consider disruptive, have turned to their cultural tradition to affirm their identity. Undoubtedly, these three cultural traditions were erected on bases profoundly religious. But the extent to which religion in our sense still influences these traditions needs to be analysed, not presumed. Even if the possibility is reasonably high in these cases, more problematic is a fourth case to which *The Economist* had devoted more discussion in the previous months, the role of 'Evangelical Christianity' in the nationalism associated with the presidential candidacy of Donald Trump. We will return to this.

Of course, religion can serve as a marker of identity, and where markers are important, religious difference can be invoked. Where it is crucial to differentiate and simple inter-religious difference is not possible, intra-religious subdivisions can be invoked; thus not Christian versus Muslim, but (as in the Middle East) Shia versus Sunni, and (as in Northern Ireland) Protestant versus Catholic, and in the past Nicaean versus Arian, or Chalcedonian versus Monophysite. It is not impossible that in such clashes, although not religious in origin, religion as a marker becomes so significant that participants are led to appropriate religious identity in a substantive sense, but this need not be so.

In the contemporary West, identity is invariably multiform, and elements of identity can vary greatly in importance, and no one element fully constitutes contemporary 'modular man'.[71] Consider this imaginary Englishman: husband, father, graduate, lawyer, Arsenal fan, cricket fanatic, Labour voter, Methodist, Wagner buff, viola player, Bugatti driver, yachtsman, treasurer of amateur dramatic society, collector of eighteenth-century porcelain. No one of those labels exhausts him, and the importance of any particular one can wax and wane. He may grow tired of the law, and turn to tulip growing on land bequeathed by an uncle. For the companionship of his new brother-in-law, he may forsake Arsenal and (however improbably) start supporting Tottenham. Because of difficulty in obtaining spare parts and the dubious character of the local dealer, he may drop Bugattis and begin driving Lamborghinis. Through the influence of the charismatic local vicar, he may turn from Methodism to Anglicanism—indeed, he may read Richard Dawkins, and come to reject all forms of Christianity. And so on—and all with minimal effect on his self-awareness. Such changes have not always been possible, especially in small, self-contained communities. In the European Middle Ages, the institutions of Catholicism were such a force in social life that one could not easily opt out, and the articulation of the Christian intellectual system was so powerful that it was virtually impossible to experience reality in any markedly different way. If in the West religion as a marker of identity has become increasingly less significant (just one possible element among all the others), this is not so everywhere. In many places, religion remains the primary (only?) source of identification. It may even be increasing in importance, often after the failure of substitutes like socialism or nationalism in parts of the Arab world. Even here, however, as noted, this falling back on 'religion as identity' may be nothing more than turning to tradition, community or ethnicity, and need not involve religion as the term is used here.

That claiming a religious identity may not primarily be related to religion at all is well illustrated (along with the complexity of interpreting polls) in an analysis of Christian identification in Britain's 2001 census. Voas and Bruce examined two anomalies. First, the census produced a much higher figure than other surveys for nominal Christian identification. Second, the census showed a higher percentage of Christians in England and Wales (72%) than in Scotland (65%) where, however, church attendance is significantly higher. They suggested an answer to both by postulating anxiety about national (rather than religious) identity. The census was conducted at a time of general concern in England and Wales about the growth and politicisation of Islam and an increase in asylum seekers. In Scotland, by contrast, there are far fewer non-Christians (less than a third of the proportion in England): 'Scottish problems with identity are much more focused on relations with the English than on the number and presence of non-Christians.'[72] The difference in census forms helped contribute to the results. First, the order of questions was not the same. In England and Wales, the religion question immediately followed those on ethnicity, thus appearing to be a supplementary question on the same topic. In Scotland, the religion question was first, 'and hence answers were arguably less "contaminated" by the desire to make it clear that "we're white and not Muslim"'.[73] Second, in England and Wales, the census form offered a single, undifferentiated 'Christian' category. This option, when contrasted with Muslim, Hindu and so on, 'must frequently have been viewed as a system of cultural classification';[74] one could cheerfully tick the 'Christian' option without having any relation to any church. In Scotland, by contrast, 'the wording (referring to "religion, religious denomination or body") and the denominational options provided made the question more evidently one on religion per se'.[75] The authors conclude that the census figures for Christians 'only make sense in the context of public concerns about national identity, expressed on a census form that was especially well suited to reveal them'.[76]

Reality

Some of the confusion in discussing religion arises from the fact that many (especially sociological) studies are conducted with only limited exposure to the reality on the ground. Maybe the study of religion was always so prone:

> De Tocqueville was probably the only member of the founding generation of sociologists to take the trouble to analyse in detail the religious affairs of his day. Comte, Saint-Simon, Spencer, Marx, Engels, Durkheim, Weber and Simmel preferred, instead, to study at best the implications that they foresaw for religion in the master trends of social change.[77]

ISSUES

Theory may not be closely related to what in fact is the case, and emphasis on one's theory may distort one's perception. An institution that has tax-free status, a huge car park, and a cross on the top of its principal building is presumed to be a church, and *therefore* concerned with God, salvation and the afterlife. As we shall see, closer acquaintance may reveal that this is often not necessarily the most helpful way to understand it; indeed, such an understanding can distort the reality on the ground.

Below we shall have something to say about 'Evangelicals' or 'Bible-believing Christians'. 'Bible-believing' is taken as a category we all know and understand, a category that conveys specific and useful information and needs no further elucidation. Yet many who readily use the word 'biblical' pay little attention to the way the Bible actually functions. Scripture, as opposed to just a holy book—so *the Bible* as distinct from Augustine or Calvin—means that the community, understanding these books *as Scripture*, is committed to find what it needs in those texts.[78] For most of history that has not been difficult. That was the whole point of figurative or allegorical interpretation; allegory can almost be defined as a method enabling one to find in a text what one needs to. But even when these figurative interpretations are discounted, it is possible to select some scriptural passages and to ignore others, in what are invariably incredibly complex sources. This is evident in the past. Milton's 700-page *Christian Doctrine* derives every statement it makes from the Bible, yet it so contradicts what were regarded as fundamental Christian beliefs that it has been calculated that under the Presbyterian Blasphemy Ordinance of 1648, it would (if published in his lifetime) have rendered him liable to five death sentences and eight terms of life imprisonment.[79] Tendentious use of the Bible is just as evident today. The literary critic Harold Bloom says of the biblical writings of Pastor W. Criswell of First Baptist Church, Dallas, and the dominant faction of the Southern Baptist Convention: 'They are not writing about the text, in any sense whatever of text, or of that text. They write about their own dogmatic social, political, cultural, moral, and even economic convictions, and biblical texts simply are quoted, with frenetic abandon, whether or not they in any way illustrate or even approach the areas where the convictions center.'[80] This applies to the more sophisticated end of the 'Bible-believing' spec-

23

trum, too. Burtchaell nicely comments on a Christian Reformed document: 'While there were numerous and attractive quotations from Scripture, the intellectual construct on which they hung was about eighteen centuries younger than the New Testament.'[81] Of course, the same is true of liberal Christians selectively picking out Isaiah, Amos and Micah.

Confusion here besets much study of Christianity globally. Jenkins has claimed Southern churches 'preach deep personal faith and communal orthodoxy, mysticism and Puritanism, all founded on clear scriptural authority'.[82] Likewise Berger: 'Almost all of Protestantism in the Global South is evangelical in character, theologically supernaturalist, and morally conservative.'[83] Yet neither of these makes any attempt to examine how this 'clear scriptural authority' or Evangelical character functions. Nigerian Pentecostals can interpret the entire Bible in terms of witches, spells and curses in a way that would be inconceivable in the West.[84] The idea that the label 'biblical' adds something definitive or clinches an argument or closes a debate is profoundly misleading.

It is the same with tithing. Stark can write of tithing as if it is no more than the fulfilment of a biblical injunction, a measure of the health of a church, and further evidence for his market theory of religion: 'If someone provides a better product, we typically assume that consumers will be willing to pay more for it.'[85] Yet tithing is much more than that. It is in many cases the motor that drives 'American religious vitality' in a way of which Stark seems completely ignorant. America's entire prosperity gospel sector (we will return to this, given its wide diffusion) depends on tithes and offerings. The aggressive, theologically driven quest for funds is the salient characteristic of many churches. How else can they afford the building programmes, affiliated colleges, even private jets?

We will return frequently to this disconnect between theory and practice, and between practice and media perception.

Method

In the course of this book I touch on various things from pilgrimage in the Middle Ages to Barack Obama's religion. My aim is not to treat these exhaustively, but to illustrate one simple point: the awareness of the otherworldly that still underpins religion almost everywhere else and has characterised the West hitherto has been largely eclipsed in the modern West, with profound consequences. I admit that in this wide sweep some of the examples will undoubtedly upset specialists in particular areas. Focus on the inadequacy of particular illustrations should not divert attention from my one simple point. Steven Weinberg, the Nobel Prize-winning physicist, notes that many mathematically obsessed physicists insist on absolute rigour; he, by contrast, demands only enough to minimise the chance of serious mistakes, and remarks in the introduction to one of his books: 'there are parts of this book that will bring tears to the eyes of the mathematically inclined reader'.[86] It is not my intention so to afflict readers, but urge concentration on my principal point.

In what follows I am talking in the realm of the general mass of people, and of a major shift of perception. In his Gifford lectures, Owen Chadwick delivered the disarming aside: 'When I say *everyone* I use it in its conventional meaning of quarter-of-the-middle-class.'[87] I accept his gentle admonition; I am well aware of the numbers who do not fit my picture, but am concerned with the overwhelming mass of the population who do. I am painting a high-level, big-screen, wide-angle picture of what I will call a major cognitive shift in the West. It is not relevant to insist 'the West' is itself a mental construct;[88] in what follows I will attempt to show that there is a cognitive style that without too much distortion can differentiate certain peoples from others.

This book deals almost exclusively with the cognitive element within religion, so exclusively that it is worth stressing at the outset that I am well aware that there is far more to religion than that. Religion has been linked to and been a vehicle of community, tradition, emotion, ritual, colour, beauty, value, art, poetry and much else. However, I here deal with these only tangentially. In discussing Western religion in the last few centuries, I hardly mention the separation between church and state (the modern state could not emerge before the dismantling of the two pillars of former society, the nobility and the church). I am making another point.

Most of the illustrative data here come from Britain or the United States. The data refer predominantly to Catholicism and Anglicanism (mainly because I am more aware of their dynamics, and, at least in the case of Catholicism, abundant official pronouncements make it easier to handle). Again, I am aware of particular trajectories outside Britain and the United States which have given rise to different attitudes to Christianity. France had its St Bartholomew's Day, its Revolution and the Dreyfus case. Italy had the Risorgimento with its need to incorporate the Papal States and take Rome as its capital. Spain had its Inquisition and the Civil War (before which, in Brenan's nice phrase, enraged Spaniards killed priests 'one might almost say in true Catholic and filial anger').[89] Poland, Ireland and Sweden likewise have their own histories, with differing roles for religion. Nevertheless, I would insist that there is value in attempting to paint an overarching trajectory which in my opinion explains the predicament of Western religion in all these countries today.

Collini, reviewing a biography of Ernest Gellner, finds that Gellner's insistence 'on a single major change in history' in large measure 'turned on the nebulous and essentially ahistorical category of "modernity" and its necessary twin, "traditional society", categories that risk barring the way to the nuanced understanding of actual historical change in a specific time and place'. Collini's limited sympathy for an enterprise like Gellner's he attributed to the fact that so much of what was of interest to him as an intellectual historian of recent centuries was, in all its richness, simply shoehorned into the capacious category of 'modernity' with the aim of showing its contrast with the 'pre-modern'.[90] Collini would find the same limitations here, expressed even more unsubtly. Nevertheless, highlighting this gulf, in the matter of religion, makes a simple point that remains hidden in much study of contemporary religion.

Matthew Arnold lamented that much of 'the blundering to be found in the world comes from people fancying that some idea is a definite and ascertained thing, like the idea of a triangle, when it is not; and proceeding to deduce properties from it, and to do battle about them, when their first start was a mistake!'[91] I can only invite students of religion to accept for the purposes of this exercise the 'definite and ascertained' idea of religion as relating to another reality, and see what insight ensues.

2

A COGNITION TRANSFORMED

My concern here is to draw attention to the major change that has affected the West in the last few centuries. I do not, however, want to imply that Western Christianity was static until then. There have been enormous and continual changes—the differences well caught in a schema like Küng's paradigms: successively the Jewish-Christian Apocalyptic, the Hellenistic Byzantine, the Medieval Scholastic, the Protestant Reformation, the Catholic Counter-Reformation, the Modern Enlightenment, the Contemporary Postmodern paradigms.[1] But all those paradigms except perhaps the last have been premised on and presupposed a personal force who has revealed his saving plan, to conform to which is our destiny on earth. All those previous paradigms have been built on awareness of the supernatural realm.

Let me illustrate this by outlining briefly (and necessarily baldly) Christianity of the High Middle Ages, that period of European history covering the 900s till about 1300.

In the world at that time, the supernatural was tangible; so God, angels, demons and saints were the really real. Just as Plato had concentrated on the eternal forms rather than the earthly things which were patterned on them, so for the tenth century it was the supernatural world, not the world of nature, which was authentic reality. The natural world was downplayed. Human beings were relatively powerless. They could survive only through their dependence on the supernatural. Surrounded by extremely harsh circumstances and an environment which they found terrifying, and 'in a situation in which so little was known about the workings of nature, it was easy for what happened to be *experienced* as a supernatural intervention'.[2] Without any technological resources on which they could rely, 'the only available ways of dealing with the situation were symbolic ways, which meant in fact resort to the supernatural'.[3]

Religion was basically concerned with saints rather than God or Jesus. The localised saint was important for his or her capacity to work miracles, and these as a result of being cajoled or manipulated, for example with gifts. These wonder-working saints were effectively seen as minor deities or demigods, and their relics seen as the main channel through which supernatural power was available for the needs of ordinary life. Relics were 'discovered' in all sorts of ways, normally through visions or dreams. Individual relics might be discredited, but opposition to relics as such was almost unheard of. The test of shrines and relics was the miracles performed at and through them. In all the medieval miracle collections, it was miraculous cures that predominated, and miracles were not restricted to breaking natural laws in David Hume's sense; a miracle was considered a normal though undoubtedly remarkable event, so perfectly natural explanations were often disregarded in favour of supernatural ones. Miracles settled everything, and it was in these miracles that the masses were primarily interested. Consequently 'it is scarcely too much to say that the popular religion of these centuries was centred not on the sacraments, not on God or the life of Christ, but on the saints and their relics'.[4]

Religion and society were closely interrelated. Society was enormously stratified into three castes—nobility, clergy, peasantry, with women and slaves effectively outside these strata.[5] Thus inequality was the first principle of reality. This reflected the social scene; the king (after the break-up of the Carolingian empire after AD 840) was more remote; the really important figure was the local lord, normally governing with total caprice, which contributed to the sense of the supernatural as arbitrary. Because of the importance of the supernatural, it was the monastic life that was regarded effectively as the primary (only?) way to salvation. Religion was what *they* performed on behalf of the rest (here we encounter genuine 'vicarious religion', a notion we will meet again). There was no Christianity adapted to the masses, for whom life was not only 'solitary, poor, nasty, brutish and short' (not least from the warlords around them and from the total inability to combat disease), but served to reinforce the conviction of their inferiority; their role was to keep their place and support the clerics and counts. The laity were at best third-class citizens of the kingdom of God. Since it was generally believed that the number saved would be few, the masses didn't really stand much chance, which did little to alleviate their sense if not of despair and hopelessness, certainly of pessimism and resignation. Thus religion wasn't simply a way of understanding the social world; it created it and reinforced it by allocating different status and (in effect) destiny.[6]

Society was uniform. Travel for most meant the next village. Tawney has actually claimed that most people in the Middle Ages would have met at most a hundred people in their entire lives, but even if he was exaggerating, there was simply little possibility of encountering and thus comparing something markedly different.[7] There was no justice system or police force or means of social control, so supernatural guidance was needed on disputed matters. Hence the institution of 'the ordeal', based on the notion of appropriateness; a just God would not let the guilty go free.[8]

Education was nonexistent except for clerics (predominantly higher clerics and monks, for the parish clergy came largely from the class of serfs).

> The clergy were the intelligentsia of the age, the only people who could explain the nature of reality and the way it worked. They were also the technologists, the only people believed capable of understanding what was going on and of producing—by their prayers and sacramental activities—the results which the age desperately needed but had not the knowledge to produce by secular means.[9]

The result of all this was that reality was actually *experienced* more or less exactly as it was pictured in the church's teaching (by then clearly elaborated, and, be it said, built on the Fathers of the church rather than anything strictly biblical; in fact, this ecclesiastical story controlled the way the Bible was understood). But even clerical learning was limited; they had few books, and *lectio divina* consisted not in seeking novelty but in reinforcing the accepted schema (because God had revealed everything already). The understanding of the past, as of the surrounding world, was from patristic theology, not empirical observation.

Diseases and afflictions, experienced as divine punishment, created and reinforced the emphasis on God's wrath; God must indeed be angry with humans, if this is what they merited. The honour of God was all-important. Reparation was required; the necessity of justice gave rise to the understanding of substitutionary penal atonement (the tensions in this understanding were simply not seen as tensions). In monastic devotion, God might be the sum of all perfections, but he was still the God of wrath, appeased by meritorious living, by penance, by the intercession of the saints, by the saying of masses and other sacramental means.[10] Merit was crucial. The ethos was basically Pelagian: you had to earn things by hardship and suffering, which could be undergone by others (although it took some time to elaborate the complete idea of Purgatory). The mass was one way of earning merit, but mass was not yet as important as it would become.

The idea of merit had profound effect on the development of pilgrimage. From the time of the early church, absolution from sin had required the performance of penitential practices, usually under the supervision of the confessor who had imposed them. 'From the end of the tenth century, however, penitents were usually absolved and reconciled with the Church immediately after confession. Thus arose the distinction between sin and punishment: the former was expunged by confession; the latter remained to be suffered in Purgatory.'[11] But the penitential system of these centuries offered only a partial solution, for by preserving an elaborate distinction between guilt and punishment, it left the sinner with most of his burden. The prospect of a second baptism, of starting spiritual life anew, became irresistibly attractive. This is what the great shrines increasingly and unashamedly offered the sinner, although the notion that a pilgrim had only to go to a particular shrine to be pardoned is scarcely found before the ninth century, and did not command universal acceptance until the eleventh.[12] It was the first crusade (AD 1095) that gave rise to the idea of the crusade as the complete and immediate ticket to salvation.[13] Simultaneously there arose the idea of indulgences. 'The rapid development of indulgences, like that of the vow of pilgrimage, owed everything to the crusades.'[14]

Indulgences encouraged the idea that merit was a commodity, and therefore transferable. The theory developed until in the thirteenth century indulgences could be applied to the dead in Purgatory, which was perhaps the cornerstone of late medieval piety.[15]

My argument is that Christianity of the Middle Ages was built on awareness of the supernatural world. Christianity was 'lived out against a strongly supernatural backdrop. Yet that hardly does justice to the situation: it was not just that people believed, in the abstract, in the existence of supernatural forces and factors which could affect things: events were actually experienced as the work of these beings.'[16]

At this point, we can take note of an argument sometimes directed against the secularisation thesis, that secularisation theorists presuppose a golden age which never actually existed.[17] Orthodox Christianity, it is claimed, was never fully appropriated; in the Middle Ages, say, few properly understood concepts like the Trinity or atonement, and in fact the majority were steeped in superstition. Medieval Christianity manifested among other things phenomena like ingesting demons through food, sexual intercourse between spirits and humans, spirit possession and exorcisms, out-of-body flight with demonic forces, the demonic insertion of foreign matter into humans, pacts with demonic agents, and rituals countering hostile sorcery.[18] The superstition can be readily admitted, but the superstition verifies the point under discussion here. It testifies further to the 'otherworldly' focus of existence. In Sumption's words: 'It is perhaps true, in the broadest possible sense, to speak of the Middle Ages as an "age of faith", but it was an age of extremely varied and heterodox faith, in which the missionary aspect of the Church's work was kept alive by ignorance and heresy.'[19] I have made much of indulgences above (and will make more below). Bruce comments:

> The habit which is often invoked as proof of the corruption of the Christian church—the sale of indulgences—actually testifies to the power of religion. People would not have paid considerable sums of money to be easily relieved of the burden of their sins if they had not believed (a) that there was a God who would punish them for those sins and (b) that the church had the power to intervene on their behalf.[20]

Thus the response of Eamon Duffy, Professor of the History of Christianity at Cambridge, to a question whether the myriad superstitions at Glastonbury today parallel the superstitions of the Middle Ages (the 'New Age' parallel often suggested, to which we will return):

> Not at all. This is different. Before the Reformation, quaint though some of the superstitions might be, there was a genuine coherence in them. All spiritual power flowed from the one God, the Incarnation, the Crucifix and the Mass. High and low beliefs were held together, so that you could draw a straight line from St Thomas Aquinas to the blessing of ploughs, from the most daring speculations about the nature of God to prayers to St Anthony for the tantony-pig, the runt of the litter. Pagan superstitions were rolled up in religious practice, as at Christmas and Easter, but they were still corralled within the disciplined coherence of Christian theology: God is one, omnipotent, omniscient, omnipresent; He gave us free will and we abused it; His son took on humanity in order to redeem all wickedness; He promises eternal life and joy to those who accept that redemption and love Him and their neighbour.[21]

All the available evidence supports the otherworldly orientation of both orthodoxy and its deviations. Of all world religions, Christianity was the one par excellence creating intellectual and institutional structures. The sophisticated intellectual framework became determinative for the perception of the otherworldly, shaping it in a predetermined way (though obviously not unfailingly), and over time Christianity's institutions became increasingly prepared to enforce the orthodoxy. The most famous deviation from orthodoxy recorded is that found in the records of the Inquisition of the early fourteenth century from Montaillou, the last outpost of the Albigensians. Their beliefs were certainly unorthodox, but everything from the myth of the fall to their beliefs about the afterlife betrays their concern with the supernatural. Their unorthodoxy consisted in their distrust of the institutions of the church to effect their eternal salvation, and hence the recourse to *perfecti* or *parfaits* who they thought could.[22]

Our key point is well expressed by Sumption:

> God appeared to control the entire natural world from moment to moment. He was the direct and immediate cause of everything that happened, from the most trivial to the most vital incidents of human life … The reactions of men when faced with what they conceived to be overpowering supernatural forces, changed remarkably little in a thousand years of Christian history.[23]

I do not intend to pile up further cases exemplifying this, but let me give two illustrations of a wrathful God's presumed agency for two cataclysmic events from almost opposite ends of this thousand-year span: the plague that fatally crippled the Roman Empire in the time of Justinian (AD 527–65), and the Black Death which killed an estimated one-third to one-half of Europe in the fourteenth century (my selection of 'cataclysmic' events is in no way meant to imply that more ordinary events were understood 'naturally').

The chronicler of Justinian's empire was Procopius, who in his *History of the Wars* begins his account of the plague: 'During these times, there was a pestilence, by which the whole human race came near to being annihilated ... for this calamity, it is quite impossible either to express in words or to conceive in thought any explanation except to refer it to God.'[24] For the Black Death, the Pope himself, in a Bull of September 1348, spoke of the 'pestilence with which God is afflicting the Christian people'. Similarly, to the Emperor John Cantacuzene, it was clear that such horrors, stenches and agony, especially one bringing despair to victims before they died, were not a plague 'natural' to mankind but 'a chastisement from Heaven'.[25]

Change

If the Christian past was marked by this awareness of the otherworldly, if the ordinary, natural and immediate way of experiencing reality was in terms of spiritual forces, it is equally evident that this is an area which has seen an enormous change. If acknowledging the shift is easy, the reasons for it are less clear. The Younger Berger points out that there is no need to find one cause ('monocausalism'), and although giving full play for the rise of science and even the religious factors involved, he prioritises social infrastructural factors.[26] For my purposes, however, I want to stress the cognitive shift associated with the rise of science, but readily admit that this shift constitutes something far more than merely cognitive, embracing social, cultural, political and economic dimensions too.

In the last few centuries, a new cognitive culture has arisen among Western elites, leading to a new way of experiencing reality generally. Calling it the scientific revolution is often disputed, and the term itself did not take hold until the 1930s. (Steven Shapin's treatment memorably begins: 'There is no such thing as the Scientific Revolution, and this is a book about it.'[27]) Nevertheless, one can say that between 1572 (the appearance of Brahe's nova) and 1704 (the publication of Newton's *Opticks*), a recognisably new consciousness emerged.[28] Reasoning ceased to be about drawing conclusions from principles, premises and authorities; it was built on observation, experiment, measurement. 'The basic difference between Galileo and his opponents was that they were philosophers, while he was a mathematician in the process of becoming a scientist.'[29] Crucially the knowledge privileged was 'useful knowledge', or knowledge through observation, experiment and mathematics ('science and technology') and contributing to the enhancement of human life (that's the significance of 'useful'). Bacon, though not a prominent scientist himself, is often credited as being a major influence here: 'Bacon's legacy was a concrete and materialistic science based on data and experiments, sharply rejecting what the age called "hypotheses" but which in our lingo would be thought of as speculation.'[30] The shift occurred across Europe, although its centre was undoubtedly Britain, and Britain was clearly the leader in the industrial revolution strictly so called, the application of this new consciousness to technological developments which came somewhat later (conventionally AD 1760–1820/40). That Europe was a network of small countries has been considered important, since someone harried for dangerous novelty could slip across the border to a more friendly clime in a way impossible for example in China—indeed, the element of competition and confrontation was as essential to this cognitive shift as was collaboration or furthering the work of others.

This new form of knowing depended upon the readiness to critique and even overturn previous authorities. In this new 'market for ideas' authorities ceased to have unquestionable status; nothing was beyond criticism. The shift thus drew considerable opposition, since it involved the downplaying of previous authorities like Galen, Plutarch, Ptolemy and, above all, Aristotle and the Bible, long considered virtually unchallengeable repositories of truth. For this reason the telescope was an instrument dangerously subversive because challenging the cosmology of the ancients; by contrast, the microscope was far less controversial because not so directly challenging them.

Obviously one of the triggers of this shift was the discovery of the new world, which at a stroke destroyed one of the planks of prior cosmology, the 'two-spheres theory' which foreclosed the possibility of any antipodes. Wootton calls the impact of these voyages 'the discovery of discovery'; it legitimated, across the board, the quest for novelty because it revealed once for all that previous authorities had not known everything.[31] Facts were facts—and theoretical considerations had to give way in the face of facts.[32] The publication of the Latin translation of Vespucci's voyages 'was the first occasion since the establishment of universities in the thirteenth century on which a philosophical theory was destroyed by a fact ... In 1507 the relationship between theory and evidence changed, and changed forever.'[33]

Education in the West changed in light of this cultural shift, which in large measure arose independent of universities and the accepted 'centres of wisdom'. In so many ways, practical or 'scientific' pursuits displaced traditional subjects of inquiry. Philosophy and theology were dethroned. A new form of education or 'human capital' became valued; fencing, literature, classical languages and games made room for accounting, chemistry, woodworking, agriculture, navigation and mechanics. New values and even a new 'morality of knowledge' arose. The Royal Society's motto *nullius in verba* (roughly, 'take no one's word for it') aptly sums up the moral component in this cognitive shift, and indeed the Society's foundation in 1660 is another key date in this evolution. This was clearly more than a mere cognitive shift; obviously printing was crucial in this market of ideas, and *intelligencers* (the intellectual go-betweens providing the links between those actually making the discoveries) were a crucial part of this.[34] This new style of knowing depended on and in turn promoted an entire social and cultural revolution.[35]

Over time, this 'useful knowledge' came to overshadow any other kind of knowledge. Moral considerations could not stand in the light of established facts. Sacred cows were sacrificed everywhere on the altar of evidence.[36] Moreover, the knowledge so gained was by definition provisional or incomplete—it was always open to be corrected in the light of new and better experiments. Progress became obvious—not in any moral sense, but in the sense that newer approaches and techniques could be more powerful and productive.[37] 'Useful knowledge' became so fruitful, continually delivering obvious benefits, that in the minds of many it came to displace any other kind of inquiry altogether. It spread beyond its geographical origins, too, affecting other parts of the globe.

This new way of knowing was not anti-religious. In fact, in its origins a religious vision may well have driven it. Building on Merton's study of Puritans at the origins of British science, Mokyr suggests that the rise of science was seen as a religious act, an act of worshipping God. [38] It was not just something secular which was religiously motivated; it was actually about discovering God's face in nature, so this new quest for new knowledge was almost a way of adoration. However, since it operated essentially on another plane, it could in time be decoupled from any religious considerations, and this was in fact what happened.

> The irony is hard to miss. Newton was a deeply religious man, for whom his findings affirmed the ever-presence of a wise deity who had created a world of knowable regularities. But Newtonian mechanical philosophy did not strictly require a personal and conscious God, and it is telling that many of his Enlightenment followers, above all Voltaire, could decouple his scientific works from his faith and adopt the former without paying much attention to the latter. [39]

The rise and increasing dominance (often to the extent of exclusivity) of this new cognitive style gave rise to modernity, a concept hard to define, but recognisable enough; the idea can be succinctly conveyed without too much distortion as this change in consciousness, from a concern with a supernatural realm to a preoccupation (not necessarily exclusive) with the this-worldly.

Although it is not our immediate concern here, there is a significant debate on the role Christianity itself played in this shift. Some forms of Christianity obviously contributed little. The reactionary stance of the Catholic Church, often in the persons of Jesuits, has been considered a block, though some would argue not to the extent often claimed. [40] Weber's idea that Calvinism played a crucial role is often invoked—and there are plenty of scholars prepared to give weight to his view. [41] However, there are others just as dubious about Weber's thesis. [42] In this shift from *Agraria* to *Industria*, Gellner gives considerable prominence to Protestantism understood generally. It did away with miracle, patronage and trickery, leading to a world considered as a stable 'nature' rather than a 'cosmos'. 'Nature' can be broken down into parts and studied as it is, unlike the 'cosmos' which in agrarian society had 'generously project[ed] purpose, hierarchy, inherent value everywhere'.[43] However, even some of those who see little value in Weber's thesis (apart from the debate to which it has given rise) can still find religion playing a role. As noted, Merton has argued that Puritanism played a large role in the rise of science in Britain. Fukuyama argues that of the three requirements for modern political order (a strong state, rule of law, accountability), the medieval church created two: celibacy gave rise to a competent bureaucracy (family ties are the big evil for Fukuyama), and canon law gave rise to transparent and predictable law. (Fukuyama is exceptional in pushing back the origins of the modern well before the early modern period.[44]) Yet there is little agreement as to why the intellectual, moral and socio-political shift occurred where and when it did. There seems a considerable element of the fortuitous in it. Gellner refers to fifteen different suggested explanations, which in some combination may provide the answer. He concludes:

> It is unlikely that we shall ever know with precision the precise path by which we have escaped from the idiocy of rural life (Karl Marx's phrase). An enormously complex, multi-faceted historical process took place: the record is fragmentary and at the same time overburdened with data. Many factors are inherently inaccessible, and the practical and conceptual problems involved in disentangling the threads will in all probability remain insoluble.[45]

The form of knowing associated with science has come to define knowledge. I would argue that the rise of this scientific consciousness (to repeat, not dissociated from conjoined social, economic and political factors) has peripheralised religion in the West. The standard objection to this argument is that science has not disproved the existence of supernatural forces, even if science must operate on atheistic assumptions. Thus Brad Gregory's insistence that methodological naturalism does not entail metaphysical naturalism.[46] But for understanding contemporary social reality, that is not really the point. The point is, as Gregory admits elsewhere, that 'Modern reason in its two most influential expressions is a schizophrenically mixed bag: philosophy has dramatically failed, but science has spectacularly succeeded',[47] and to such a degree that already by the end of the nineteenth century, 'the success of the natural sciences had made their epistemology the paradigm for knowledge as such'.[48] It may not be a matter *of necessity*, but *in fact* more and more people in the West seem to have grown so used to understanding causality on the natural plane that they see no need to go further. For example, when malaria is identified as the cause of death, most in the West see no need to inquire further about the malign force that led this particular mosquito to bite that particular individual; bad luck, or carelessness, or statistical probability is a sufficient explanation. Gregory's singling out Occam's razor (*entia non sunt multiplicanda praeter necessitatem*) as a major factor contributing to contemporary intellectual confusion doesn't alter the fact that it seems to have become part of Western consciousness.[49]

David Martin has written: 'Truths are not all of a kind. The temperature at which water boils is a truth different in kind from a claim to *be* the Way, the Truth and the Life, or all that is conveyed by Titian's final Pieta or his *Noli me tangere*.'[50] Yes, very true, but most peoples of the world have muddled through in ignorance of Martin's second and third truths; by contrast, that water boils at 100 degrees Celsius at sea level is a truth so incontrovertible, so repeatable, and so demonstrably beneficial, that for many it constitutes for better or worse something of a gold standard.

Collingwood summed up this cognitive revolution:

> Soon after the beginning of (the seventeenth) century, a number of intelligent people in western Europe began to see in a settled and steady manner what a few here and there had seen by fits and starts for the last hundred years or more: namely that the problems which ever since the time of early Greek philosophy had gone by the collective name of "physics" were capable of being restated in a shape in which, with the double weapon of experiment and mathematics, one could now solve them.[51]

Collingwood does not say that this double weapon of experiment and mathematics could solve all problems, nor that no other weapons existed, but his words explain why so many might infer that.

Nor is it a telling objection that this new way of knowing cannot explain or justify in full what it is doing. Wootton is clear: 'We cannot provide a satisfactory philosophical justification for these types of knowledge (broadly, "the sciences"), but we can tell that they work.'[52]

Weinberg admits the holes in scientific method: 'There is active and interesting work on the philosophy *of* science, but it has very little effect on scientific research.'[53] Science, for him, is better explained as a tangle of deduction, induction and guesswork; or 'guesswork, guided by aesthetic judgment, and validated by the success of many of its predictions'.[54] That is sufficient for Gellner, too: 'Our cognitive activities can at best stumble upon truth by accident.'[55] Although the scientific approach may not be able to justify itself philosophically, it has justified itself by undermining all previous systems and carrying all before it.

Similarly, the lament that science cannot answer the really important human questions largely misses the reality of Western life today. Science has advanced by avoiding questions that apparently lead nowhere and by formulating questions that may fruitfully be addressed: 'The progress of science has been largely a matter of discovering what questions should be asked.'[56] This fact, I suggest, is largely responsible for the increasing reluctance to ask the 'ultimate questions' so loved by philosophers and theologians. Again, there is no reason why people should *not* ask what are considered 'deeper' questions; the fact remains, however, that, given the incompatibility of the various answers on offer, many seem to think that there is little advantage to be had in going down that path. (The pernicious nature of some of the ultimate answers most prominent today has probably only reinforced such reluctance.) One may rail against, say, affluence, professional sport, mass travel, the consumer society or a culture of instant gratification, which all prevent people asking deeper questions, but the reality remains that many no longer feel any pressing need to do so.

My point is that the modern Western world increasingly operates on a plane where spiritual forces are scarcely relevant. The middle class represents for the first time in history 'not merely a class that has generally lost its faith, but rather one whose practice and whose thought, whatever its formal religious belief, are *fundamentally* irreligious in a critical area [i.e. the economy], and totally alien to the category of the sacred'.[57] Eagleton comments: 'The faithlessness of advanced capitalism is built into its routine practices. It is not primarily a question of the piety or skepticism of its citizens. The marketplace would continue to behave atheistically even if every one of its actors was a born-again Evangelical.'[58] What is true of capitalism is just as true of the fields of

technology and bureaucracy, which bring their own form of consciousness which simply leaves aside the supra-empirical. In *The Homeless
Mind* Berger and his co-authors analyse modernity in terms of technology and bureaucracy. Technology entails mechanisticity, reproducibil-
ity, measurability. These qualities of technology give rise to a 'cognitive
style' which includes componentiality (or perceiving the world as
made of units that can be dismantled and rearranged), separability of
means and ends, abstract and preferably quantitative thinking, prob-
lem-solving inventiveness, assumption of maximalisation, positive valuing of innovation, segregation of work from private life, anonymous
social relations, and multi-relationality (or an ability to deal with many
things at once). Likewise, bureaucracy functions through competence,
referral, coverage, proper procedure, access to redress, and anonymity.
The 'cognitive style' that necessarily flows from this bureaucratic functioning comprises orderliness, general and autonomous organisability,
predictability, a general expectation of justice, moralised anonymity
and explicit abstraction. Thus a society structured through technology
and bureaucracy carries with it a particular cognitive style. An individual socialised into such a society absorbs this cognitive style, operates in terms of a 'modern' worldview, where explanations in terms of
otherworldly forces simply have no place. [59]

Many are prepared to push this idea to its limit. Gellner insists we
learn through experience and we learn in no other way. [60] This attitude
is found more widely. Mencken writes of metaphysics with his typical
dismissiveness: 'A metaphysician is one who when you remark that
twice two makes four, demands to know what you mean by twice,
what by two, what by makes, and what by four. For asking such questions metaphysicians are supported in oriental luxury in the universities, and respected as educated and intelligent men.' [61] But universities
can undermine metaphysics, too. Hugh Trevor-Roper, almost the
embodiment of the Oxford academic at the apogee of its intellectual
confidence and social standing, comments that during a walk in 1936,
'pondering on the complicated subtleties of St Augustine's theological
system, which I had long tried to take seriously, I suddenly realised the
undoubted truth that metaphysics are metaphysical, and having no
premises to connect them to this world, need not detain us while we
are denizens of it. And at once, like a balloon that has no moorings, I

saw the whole metaphysical world rise and vanish out of sight in the upper air, where it rightly belongs; and I have neither seen it, nor felt its absence, since.'[62] And A.J. Ayer, the personification of the view that only science and experience have meaning, in his autobiography makes a statement which gives some idea of how widely it has spread:

> I still broadly adhere to what may be called the verificatory approach. So indeed does a great deal of subsequent philosophy, though the fact is not often recognised. The verification principle is seldom mentioned and when it is mentioned it is usually scorned; it continues, however, to be put to work. The attitude of many philosophers towards it reminds me of the relation between Pip and Magwitch in Dickens's *Great Expectations*. They have lived on the money, but are ashamed to acknowledge its source.'[63]

It is hard to disagree with *The Economist* when it remarked in an editorial on how science has revolutionised human life both intellectually and practically:

> That the mental landscape today is almost unrecognisable from that of, say, two centuries ago, is due almost entirely to the work of two groups of thinkers: scientists and economists. Add engineers to that list and you have an explanation for why the physical, commercial and political landscapes have changed just as radically.[64]

This change in consciousness, it is my argument, has driven the awareness of the supernatural to the periphery. Science has not 'disproved' religion. Science and religion are not engaged in some zero-sum struggle; that claim is often given more attention than it merits, for it is largely a red herring.[65] But it is almost impossible in the West today to experience the supernatural in the taken-for-granted manner of the past. Those affected by this change experience reality in a way different from that of previous ages, because tending to bypass (if not necessarily deny) the ubiquitous superhuman forces hitherto taken for granted and commonly considered the foundation of religion. On the topic of *The Supernatural in Tudor and Stuart England*, Oldridge writes: 'The intellectual, social and physical environment overwhelmingly encouraged the acceptance of otherworldly powers. It is one measure of this fact that the contemplation of the natural world led routinely to the confirmation of supernatural beliefs, just as today it provides evidence of scientific naturalism.'[66] Exactly. As late as the Tudors and

Stuarts, people in Britain experienced reality in terms of otherworldly forces, and their everyday experience reinforced that perception. We don't, and our everyday experience reinforces a markedly different worldview. This has unavoidably affected Western churches. I referred above to the Black Death of 1347–51. Contrast the English Church's response to that with its response to the HIV/AIDS 'gay plague' of the 1980s. 'In the first, the Church called for weeks of fasting and special prayers. In the second, it called for more government investment in medical/scientific research.'[67] There is summed up the plight of the Christian churches today. Institutions built on the taken-for-granted-ness of the otherworldly have lost that rationale. 'Above all', writes Weinberg, 'we must not imagine that our predecessors thought the way we think, only with less information.'[68]

Elsewhere

I have argued that this peripheralisation of the superhuman or non-empirical is characteristic of modernity in the West. This book is about religion in the West, and I do not want to depart too far from this focus, but I will emphasise this contrast by a brief look at a different culture where the otherworldly remains the *realissimum*.[69]

Let me briefly describe African Traditional Religion (the term is not perfect, but in the interests of brevity, let it stand). The traditional religious understanding or 'enchanted religious imagination' considers that reality is a unified whole, boundaries are fluid and permeable between what we would call the natural and the supernatural, between the human and spirit world, between humans and animals, between human and nature. Spiritual forces pervade the universe. These spirits dwell in rocks, rivers, trees, animals and objects. Indeed, nothing is purely matter, since spirits infuse everything. As already admitted, calling these forces 'supernatural' is loaded in that it requires a clear distinction between natural and supernatural that not all peoples share, nowhere better illustrated than in Lienhardt's discussion of Dinka religion, where the powers in question, far from belonging to another world, may be experienced as closer and more intimate even than members of one's own family; these spirits are the principal and most tangible forces of *this* world.[70] The human individual experiences and understands him- or herself as part of the cosmic whole. Causality is to be discerned primarily in the spiritual realm, though natural causality is not entirely disregarded. A stronger or higher spirit can easily destroy or impair a weaker or lower, and since humans rank relatively low they can be controlled by the former. This may affect one's whole family, clan or state. Spirits may be manipulated by others, particularly to inflict evil; hence the preoccupation with witchcraft (another unsatisfactory term, but again let it stand). 'Healer-diviners' exist to identify and control these pervasive spiritual forces. Religion consists largely in protecting oneself from malign spiritual powers. The absence of destructive spirits forms the idea of the good life.[71]

This worldview is pervasive. Consider some random recent examples of these supernatural agents or spiritual powers. Albinism is a melanin deficiency that leaves sufferers vulnerable to cancer. The incidence in Europe and North America is one in 20,000 persons, but in East Africa it is reckoned to be 500 per cent higher, about one in 4,000. Tanzania is estimated to have about 200,000 albinos. In late 2008 reports emerged that about 35 albinos had been killed in Tanzania that year (unreported cases were probably much higher). The reason was the belief that albino body parts through their spiritual potency can help politicians win elections, make businessmen fantastically rich overnight, cure infertility and ward off evil spirits. The demand was particularly strong among the fishing people around the south of Lake Victoria, and the alluvial miners in the gold and diamond fields south of the lake. The Tanzanian government appointed an albino woman to parliament to protect albinos' rights. In early 2009 the police chief in Dar es Salaam distributed mobile phones to several hundred albinos, with a direct line to the police, to be used if they thought they were being tracked by body-harvesters. The problem continues. In 2013, the UN High Commissioner for Human Rights deplored a recent outbreak of albino killing in Tanzania—four in the first two weeks of February.[72] In central Africa, in Gabon, the Association for the Prevention of Ritual Crimes denounced the twenty ritual murders in the early months of 2013.[73] So too in the west of the continent, in Senegal, in the run-up to the 2012 general elections, mysterious deaths were widely seen as ritual human sacrifice for success in the elections; children were warned not to go home from school unaccompanied, and albinos were considered to be in particular danger.[74] In the legislative assembly, just after the elections, a deputy shouted across to the benches of the previous government: 'Since you have lost power, albinos sleep in peace and we no longer find human remains in the streets.'[75] Nobody asked: What was he saying? What did that mean? Everyone knows full well. There is no need to pile up further examples, but to bring home the prevalence of this enchanted religious imagination: a recent United Nations report claims that in the Central African Republic, 25% of all cases brought to court in the capital Bangui, and 80–90% in CAR's rural courts, concern witchcraft. As a result 70% of prisoners in Bangui's central prison are there on the basis of witchcraft accusations.[76]

To see this enchanted imagination in daily life, let me briefly describe religion in Senegal, where I lived between 2009 and 2015.[77] Senegalese tend to see spiritual forces operative everywhere, and understand causality primarily in spiritual terms, and worldly events as determined primarily in the spiritual realm (the realm of *la mystique*). These forces can be manipulated by individuals gifted with such powers, whose services are available to those who seek them. A *marabout* is someone who claims power over the sacred and symbolic forces affecting our lives; *maraboutage* is the use of this power.

The most common kinds of *maraboutage* are aimed at the following: to enjoy prosperity, status and popularity; to control another (particularly in amatory matters, or for extracting money); to restrict another's physical movement; to cause division between others (from jealousy, or revenge, or material interest); to render oneself invisible (so one might, for example, pass through border controls unobserved); to cause sickness or death at a distance; to avoid blows or attacks on one's person; to obtain general protection from malevolent others; to send another into exile or vagabondage, or, by contrast, to bring another back to the country; to find love; to make someone impotent on his marriage night;[78] to drive someone to death or suicide. To use *maraboutage* to ensure the health, harmony and prosperity of one's family on the face of it seems something positive. However, often there is a downside: working to ensure promotion can entail the failure or firing of a competitor. To find love may mean eliminating rivals—especially in a polygamous society where *maraboutage* is often used to discredit, render infertile or ensure dismissal of a co-wife.

A COGNITION TRANSFORMED

Even if *maraboutage* can be practised anywhere, there are some places which have an aura or charge that makes them particularly suitable: places like trees, offices, crossroads, beds, lintels, markets, morgues, wells, anthills. Some of these, of their nature, lend themselves to negative *maraboutage* (morgues, cemeteries), some to positive (most notably the mosque). Some can lead in either direction: trees, with fruit, sap, foliage and roots, can possess a positive charge, but because they are considered the abode of spirits or *djinns*, also negative. Wells, with associations of life-giving water, can lead in positive directions, but the hidden, cold, dark associations can also lead in negative directions.

In all cases, the *marabout* lays down specific and particular requirements: some concoctions (requiring ingredients like powder, roots, salt, sugar, perfume to be mixed in various ways), objects (knives, nails, needles, rings, coins), bones or other parts of animals (even humans)—often made into talismans or *gris-gris*. In all *maraboutage* there is normally a certain objective or subjective resemblance between what is sought and what is used. A part can represent the whole, and to act on a part is considered to be acting on the whole, and to act on something representing the person is considered acting on the person himself. Objects can be used in various ways, like baths, potions, lotions. Sacrifices of all sorts (camels, cattle, sheep, chickens) are common, and offerings are essential, both to begin negotiations with the *marabout* and to ensure the success of the process. Failure to observe the most minute of these stipulations can cause the process to fail (constituting something of an escape: it is effectively impossible to falsify the process).

There is nothing private about this enchanted religious imagination; it pervades the public sphere. Senegal's national sport, *lutte avec frappe*, more popular than football, is as much a 'mystical' contest between the wrestlers' *marabouts* as a physical contest between the wrestlers themselves. In the build-up to the bout, their *marabouts* (sometimes up to fifty) are everywhere, and at the bout itself the wrestlers are bedecked with *gris-gris* containing protective barks and other substances, and douse themselves with protective liquids. The father of the victorious grand champion in 2013 admitted he had paid 'at least' 50 million fcfa (US$100,000) to *marabouts* to ensure his son's success[79]—an insight into the economics of *maraboutage*, a topic in itself. It is just as obvious in football. In February 2012, Senegal went

45

to the Africa Cup of Nations in Gabon–Equatorial Guinea among the favourites, but were immediately eliminated, losing all three preliminary games, and by the same score of 1–2. It was widely said that *la mystique* had caused the team's downfall.[80] In politics this religious imagination is obtrusive. When Macky Sall won Senegal's 2012 presidential election, he took some months to move into the presidential palace—a reluctance invariably attributed to the need to 'de-mine' the entire palace of the charms planted there to undermine him. In the words of one knowledgeable academic, the presidential palace is the 'most *marabouté*-ed place in Senegal, crammed with mystical bombs, offensive and defensive devices, weapons of every kind, liquid and solid, an entire sophisticated arsenal of amulets and magic charms, buried, suspended, defused in the tiniest cracks'.[81] Finding *gris-gris* planted to harm others is frequently reported. Thus a government minister received a new office chair which contained hidden *gris-gris*, obviously put there by political enemies. It is widely accepted that show business is full of *maraboutage*.

Above all, it is in the law courts where this enchanted imagination can be seen in all its variety. Some court cases deal with the killing or punishment of alleged witches, others with the protests of those so accused. Of most interest are the cases involving false *marabouts* or charlatans, which provide ample evidence of this pervasive religious imagination on which charlatans can play. To give just one example, one Senegalese woman in Italy found a *marabout* through the internet, who promptly told her that seven *djinns* threatened to kill her. The *marabout* promised to ensure a complete cure at the cost of 500,000 fcfa (US$1,000), which eventually became 1.6 million fcfa ($3,000), and which after becoming disillusioned she attempted to reclaim.[82] The cases are frequent and surprise nobody. Since about 90% of Senegalese profess to be Muslim, Senegal's *maraboutage* necessarily assumes an Islamic face, and virtually all *marabouts* would claim to be members of Sufi brotherhoods, but this is obviously a particularly enchanted form of Islam. Such is effectively the lived religion of all classes in Senegal, and I would suggest this religious imagination is found widely in Africa, not least among those identifying themselves as Christian or Muslim. It is the eclipse of that way of experiencing reality that has befallen the West, with profound effects on the institutions built on it.

3

WESTERN RELIGION TODAY

I have argued that an awareness of the supernatural or superhuman or otherworldly has receded to the very periphery of Western consciousness in recent centuries. This awareness, I maintain, underpinned and gave shape to Western Christianity in the past. With its eclipse, Western Christianity has suffered considerable attrition. Secularisation theory draws attention to various elements in this eclipse of religion in the West. Proponents of the secularisation thesis, however, argue principally from affiliation and attendance; they provide statistics for the declining number who belong to churches, and the declining number who attend services. I want to focus rather on the rationalisation element or the matter of consciousness or belief, which, as remarked above, receives far less attention, and what attention it receives can be breathtakingly blunt.

The persistence of belief

There have been notable attempts to suggest that belief is alive and well. The first is the 'believing but not belonging' notion associated with Grace Davie.[1] This insists that people still believe even if they have ceased to belong or attend. After all, it is said, drawing on Putnam's thesis of decline of association (expressed in his famous catchphrase 'bowling alone'), membership of all civic bodies from political parties to women's institutes has declined precipitously over the same period. So the fact that Christians no longer belong to or attend churches is not to be wondered at, and doesn't necessarily mean that belief is in retreat. Davie treats two main examples: trades union membership and attendance at football matches. Bruce examines the relevance of the Putnam thesis and Davie's two examples. He argues that they are not revealing parallels; trades unions in Britain have been curtailed by law, and their catchment has shrunk. Football has had 'effective substitutes'—for example, watching on TV with mates at home or in the pub. So the parallels are hardly conclusive. In her response, Davie makes much of her claim that people are not becoming less religious, but in fact more religious in an individualistic sort of way. Although Bruce insists that all research shows that beliefs have diminished alongside affiliation and attendance, assuming (probably rightly) 'churchgoing is a reasonable indicator of interest or faith in what the churches represent', both his broad assumption and Davie's counter-insistence about belief 'in an individualistic sort of way' take us not much further in establishing the content of any belief.[2]

The second notion is 'vicarious religion', also associated with Grace Davie. The examples she makes much of are the funeral of Princess Diana in August 1997, and the 1995 funeral in Notre-Dame for France's President Mitterrand.[3] The popular demand for these strongly religious ceremonies, performed by the nation's highest religious functionaries, shows, argues Davie, that religion is still strong, but the majority leave performing it to the professionals. But surely this is misleading. Both Britain and France have historically marked the death of kings and queens with massive pomp. How else would one mark the death of Princess Diana, who for two decades had virtually personified Britain's monarchy? And where else but Westminster Abbey? Wembley Stadium perhaps? The Albert Hall? Although Mitterrand was known not to be a Christian, how else could France mark the passing of someone probably of more influence than all but a few of the kings that have been buried from Notre-Dame? Surely the more prosaic reality is that both secularising Britain and the positively *laïque* French Republic have simply not evolved replacement mechanisms to perform the solemn functions developed for what were once unashamedly Christian states.[4]

I will not spend more time on 'believing but not belonging' or 'vicarious religion' because neither idea even professes to have much to say on the nature of Christian belief in today's world. More significantly, both easily link with the not unrelated idea of the 'counterculture' or 'New Age'. This is a third argument against the secularisation thesis, that although people may be less inclined to belong to or attend churches, they are devising the new forms of religion evidenced in the New Age or counterculture. The most detailed study is that by Heelas and Woodhead of the town of Kendal in the north of England, in which they examined everything that could possibly count as New Age through extensive interviews and surveys. Activities ranged from yoga, massage, homeopathy, complementary health groups, and reiki or spiritual healing. For Heelas and Woodhead their findings disprove the secularisation thesis; for Bruce, on the other hand, these findings support it. As Bruce shows, few of the activities examined are 'spiritual' in any sense at all; these include yoga, tai chi, dance, singing, and art. Massage and 'bodywork' are simply 'pampering'. Not all the 'complementary health groups' are obviously 'spiritual'; some healing activities are underpinned by distinctive ideas, but homeopathy and reiki are more pseudoscientific than 'spiritual'. Bruce notes that one doesn't have to speculate on respondents' understanding of these activities, because Heelas and Woodhead specifically asked them how they understood these practices. Less than half the respondents saw anything 'spiritual' at all in their activities. It is hard to dispute Bruce's conclusion: 'Taking New Age spirituality at its narrowest, it is trivial. In order to get over 1% of the population, we need to encompass a variety of imported recreational activities, miscellaneous methods of relaxation, and diverse forms of alternative medicine, all practised mainly by people who do not even pretend to see them as spiritual. Rather than seeing the New Age as compensating for a decline in Christianity, we should see it as an extension of the surgery, the clinic, the gym, or the beauty salon. It is primarily concerned with physical and psychological wellbeing.'[5]

Bruce's central argument is the sociological one that this 'individualised religion' has no possibility of reproducing itself, so in no way does it compensate for the decline of 'organised' religion. But given that he operates from a substantive understanding of religion, he could have gone much further and made plainer that most of this is not religion at all. (As already noted, Heelas and Woodhead have an extremely elastic understanding of religion, being prepared to understand activi-

ties as religious even in the case of somebody who insists they are not.)
Far from a new form of religion complementing or displacing older
traditional religion, the new practices represent activity on a totally
different plane. The New Age spirituality focuses on self-fulfilment,
self-expression and self-realisation, maximising potential, recognising
innate talents, projecting goals, thinking positively, heightening ambi-
tion. The focus is on finding oneself, with the self the arbiter of what is
significant and true. The spirituality is subjectivised, personalised,
therapeutic. This is profoundly different from traditionally recognisable
religion: discovering the divine will, seeking to know and fulfil this will
for the achievement of eternal salvation. The psychologised and therapeutic practices that make up the New Age do not really bear on
debates about religion in my sense.[6]

The same seems true in the United States. Woodward covered all
aspects of the 'counterculture' in his nearly forty years at *Newsweek*. In
a chapter entitled 'Experiential Religion' he covers all manifestations
of Zen, Hinduism, Buddhism, Krishna Consciousness, Transcendental
Meditation, and their mutations. Using the term 'designer Buddhism',
Woodward emphasises that what Americans adopt is not necessarily the
Buddhism practised in the East, and they understand such practices
essentially as ways to self-realisation.[7] In a further chapter on
'Alternatives to Religion' (we have already noted that Woodward
makes no attempt to clarify what he means by religion, so the reader is
not perfectly clear what would constitute an alternative), he plots the
triumph of the therapeutic, giving considerable importance to Erik
Erikson's model of psychological development, leading to the 'human
potential movement' stemming from the Esalen Institute of Big Sur,
California, which welcomed every sense-enhancing technique, every
form of ritual dynamics, every explanation of 'what life is really about'
except those derived from Christianity or Judaism.[8] The movement
culminated in Werner Erhard's EST, 'the slickest and most lucrative
package of instant self-improvement on the human potential market'.[9]
There is no reason, of course, why someone who indulges in these
practices should not do so with respect to an otherworldly realm (the
'finding the divine within oneself' may genuinely relate to the divine),
but it is clear that they are normally a search for self-discovery, self-
realisation and personal growth. This is why Berger's repudiation of the

secularisation thesis 'because of the counterculture' is confused; he, like Bruce, states explicitly that he is operating from a substantive understanding of religion; if religion is understood in this way, the counterculture has no necessary bearing on any debate on religion.

Without labouring the point, it is worth citing Harold Bloom's very idiosyncratic but stimulating study *The American Religion*, which argues that America's real religion is typically a fusion of Enthusiasm, Gnosticism and Orphism (Orphism being 'an esoteric mystery cult whose central teaching was the potential divinity of the elitist self').[10] Bloom calls the New Age 'California Orphism'. The Californian God's 'perpetual and universal immanence makes it difficult for a newager to distinguish between God and any experience whatsoever, but then why should such a distinction occur to a California Orphic?' Bloom notes that most New Agers 'hedge the obsessive immanence of God with a touch of transcendence'. But he tellingly adds, with an awareness of the lived experience that escapes so many scholars of religion, this hedging 'makes so little difference, on a daily basis, as not to survive the prag-matic test'.[11] The New Age will not feature further here, although we will later take up a notion suggested by Bloom: 'Christianity … is mostly irrelevant to the New Age, except in so far as Christianity already has been modified into the American religion, of which the New Age is sometimes a charming parody.'[12]

The distinction is well captured here:

> The novel epistemological principle [is] that the believer is the final arbiter of what is true "for her" … This is, of course, a very long way from the epistemological foundation of the major world religions, which assume that there is a God or Gods, whose will is knowable through clear but limited channels controlled by the properly appointed officials.[13]

Christian origins, therefore …

A fourth approach purportedly discrediting the secularisation thesis highlights the Christian origins of so much of Western modernity; therefore, it is insinuated (and sometimes stated explicitly), Christianity is alive and well in the West today.

The classic study of this genre is Siedentop's *Inventing the Individual*.[14] Siedentop argues that St Paul built on the Jewish stress on will (rather than the classical world's stress on reason), and thus introduced notions of the individual, equality and personal conscience. This gave rise to the notion of inwardness, and a new conception of community, and with it a new form of social organisation, namely monasticism, consisting 'of self-governing societies founded, at least in principle, on consent, and working under a rule that recognized the moral equality of brothers'.[15] After the break-up of Charlemagne's kingdom, reforms stemming from the monastery of Cluny (founded AD 910) spread to the papacy, the only candidate to lead these reforms further. The papacy came to be dominated by monks and then by canon lawyers. Canon law marked a total revolution in legal thinking, based on the individual, moral status, and natural rights.[16] 'Before the papal revolution spiritual and temporal authority in Europe had been so mixed as to be difficult to separate ... the papal revolution changed that. It pointed towards the de-sacralizing of kingship and of all secular government. It was in that sense that the church created the secular realm.'[17]

Christianity, argues Siedentop, both its ideas and institutions, thus created key elements of our world. Secularism, or 'that belief in an underlying or moral equality of humans implies that there is a sphere in which each should be free to make his or her own decisions, a sphere of conscience and free action'.[18] In time, this idea floated free of its roots and could be used against the institution that gave rise to it: 'The egalitarian moral intuitions generated by the church began to be turned against the church itself, creating misgivings that eventually led to a principled rejection of any coercive or "privileged" role for the church ...'.[19] So ideas and realities characterising our world have now become independent or free-standing.

A markedly similar approach, but on a wider and necessarily less detailed canvas, is evident in Spencer's *The Evolution of the West*. Spencer goes beyond Siedentop's concern with the individual to cover nationhood, Magna Carta, democracy, humanism, atheism, our 'scientific culture', human rights, the welfare state.[20]

Spencer does not argue that Christianity *caused* these things, much less uniquely caused them. He is aware of the complexity of the process leading to realities we recognise today, a process in which Christianity played a considerable role, though often ambiguous or unintended.[21] The most natural way of reading Spencer, as reading

Siedentop, is that these realities have floated free of their origins: for example, '[The self] might have been a distinctly Christian doctrine in its early incarnations ... but it didn't appear to be necessarily Christian.'[22] However, one sometimes gets the impression that Spencer goes further to suggest that because it played a role in creating these things, both through key concepts and as an institution, Christianity is still necessary to ground and maintain them. He explicitly argues this in regard to human rights: 'It is perhaps precisely because of that che-quered, or complex relationship that it is worth integrating serious Christian theological reflection when thinking about the foundation and future for human rights.'[23] More typically, though, he suggests that Christianity should contribute to further evolution of these realities, presumably in much the same way as other pressure groups like Human Rights Watch, Liberty, the Commission for Racial Equality.

This, of course, is to admit secularisation. Yet Spencer repeats the accepted wisdom that secularisation theory is passé:

> The secularization thesis ground to a halt at some point in the last quarter of the twentieth century, as the rest of the world veered off Europe's tracks and modernized without losing their religion, and the more muscularly religious emerged from the darkness to batter down the secular defences that the West had erected around itself.[24]

This is confused. Spencer does not see that the claim that 'most of the world' is modern in terms required by the secularisation thesis needs demonstration, and that the 'muscular religious' in particular come arguably from societies that are far from modernised—contrib-uting to their muscularity.[25]

Cupitt takes this Christian-origins-therefore approach to its limit. Whereas for Siedentop Christianity gifted the modern world with secularity,[26] for Cupitt secularity is what Christianity was about all along. So Christianity is alive and well; it is what the West has become.[27] He states, 'The emergent West is simply Christianity itself. It has com-pleted its "historical", disciplinary and ecclesiastical period and is now coming into its fulfilment.'[28] 'The modern secular West is simply Christianity in its final secularized, humanistic, third-millennium, "Kingdom" form.'[29]

A variation on this theme, which in terms of my argument here simply heaps confusion on confusion, is Erdozain's claim that since the modern secular world is caused by Christianity itself, secularisation is simply wrong and the term should be avoided. 'Fierce Christian apologists, and even fiercer "new atheists", share a common root system. Indeed the ferocity directed against religion in public life is to no small degree a product of it: a pointed and articulated fury that bears little resemblance to any hard-wired "process of secularization".'[30] His main thesis is that the roots of today's atheism lie not in a clash with science, but moral outrage against orthodox Christianity. He makes the point, especially for Bayle, Franck, Castellio, Spinoza, Voltaire and the Victorians, that their attacks on religion stemmed not from simple unbelief, but from spiritual protest that Christianity was not Christian enough. He argues that the key plank discrediting Christianity was not scientific rationality; the rage against orthodox Christianity (in particular Calvin's Augustinianism) did that. Thus: 'Calvin played a larger part in the Victorian crisis of faith than Darwin.'[31]

Yet for all the insight into key thinkers, the overall effect is confusion. Repeatedly he suggests that this contemporary unbelief is religious (or at least that since its roots are religious we can't say it is non-religious). 'One of the claims of this [Erdozain's] book is that such a dichotomy between "religious" and "secular" thought is unsustainable.'[32] Again: 'One of my claims is that modernity has been characterized by the internalization of religious ideas, not their disintegration.'[33] However, surely, to say that present unbelief had religious roots is different from saying that today's unbelief is itself religious.[34]

It is also misleading, as I have shown, to argue:

> A visceral sense of right and wrong, rather than a scientific or historical suspicion of supernatural truth claims, has served as the primary solvent of orthodoxy in the West. Christianity has generated its own critique—the process consistently overlooked by a historical perspective that reads the cause from the outcome, locating the origins of unbelief in a rational scientific consciousness that is somehow taken for the reality of the present.[35]

These authors have well shown that Christianity played a large part in the creation of Western modernity; it would be hard to claim otherwise, given its historical dominance in Western culture. However, 'It is one thing to maintain that there is a relationship of historical causality between Christianity and certain features of the modern world. It is an altogether different matter to say that, "therefore," the modern world, including its secular character, must be seen as some sort of logical realization of Christianity'.[36]

The Victorian decline

There is a considerable literature about the crisis of Christianity in Victorian times—Matthew Arnold's 'melancholy, long, withdrawing roar'. The shift has been plotted in the personal lives of intellectuals like Arnold, George Eliot and Lewes, Jowett, Spencer, Darwin, Ruskin (and behind them the Germans: Hegel, Strauss and Feuerbach). But just as important was the observable shift in the consciousness of ordinary people. Owen Chadwick expresses it: 'The forties was the time of doubts, in the plural and with a small d … In the sixties Britain and France and Germany entered the age of Doubt, in the singular and with a capital D.'[37] Newman's life illustrates this general shift. With all his undoubted brilliance, Newman was essentially a spokesman for the old order. In his *Apologia*, written in 1864 and covering his life up to 1845, he displays all his resistance to the modern world.[38] Newman totally rejects modern historiography.[39] In a note on liberalism, he makes it clear that what he is objecting to is the setting aside of tradition.[40] He's also very wary of the contribution of science,[41] yet, as I have argued, acceptance of science and its resulting technology is almost a definition of the modern world. Newman drew immense acclaim with his *Apologia*, yet, in Young's words, when Newman died in 1890 'it was in an age less concerned to know whether Newman's faith or some other faith was the right one, than whether in the modern world there was any room for faith at all'.[42]

The triggers for the crisis of religion were geology and German historical scholarship. The bestselling novel of the 1880s was Mrs Humphry Ward's *Robert Elsmere*, which charted their effects in the life of a Church of England clergyman. The eponymous cleric was symbolic of the great many clergymen who gradually thought themselves into Unitarianism (or effectively such) and social involvement. Elsmere moves into a natural form of Christianity: Christ the exemplar for the West, and embodiment of God as we all can be. He resolves for himself the issue of the miraculous, by claiming that it was essential in getting

Christianity off the ground, but by the Victorian age it was proving the greatest hindrance to acceptance. He brings his social Christianity to the East End of London. The fact that his wife continued to hold ortho-dox Christian doctrines provides much of the tension in the novel. That this bestseller is virtually unread today is an indication that concerns in precisely that form no longer exist.[43]

The moral element in this crisis gave rise to the issue of the 'ethics of belief' associated with W.K. Clifford. Clifford, a charismatic and by all accounts a loveable genius, was one of the founders of a Metaphysical Society which included most of the prominent thinkers of the day, including Catholics like Manning and Ward (Newman did not belong; his *Grammar of Assent* was arguably written as a riposte to the society's deliberations). Most of these intellectuals, including Clifford, had begun life as Christians. (Not Mill, however: 'I am thus one of the very few examples, in this country, of one who has not thrown off religious belief, but never had it.'[44]) The context for this morality debate was the wealth, property and influence of the estab-lished church. Science was in the ascendant as the new way of think-ing, yet Anglicanism and theology had a stranglehold on academic life in England. More and more people were giving up the supernatural aspects of religion. 'The question which the Zulu convert put to Bishop Colenso: Do you believe all that? could not be evaded for ever.'[45] But even those ceasing to hold to orthodox Christianity were terrified that society would collapse without an ethical base. Hence the considerable hesitation, dissembling and ambivalence characteris-ing the clergy themselves.[46] Orthodox Christianity was thus seen by many as a great impediment to intellectual advance. It was wrong to continue to promote what had been discredited. Official Christianity was immoral. There was an ethics of belief.[47]

Young's *Portrait of an Age* brilliantly captures the dynamics here. Mentally situating himself in 1900, comparing the three decades before with the three decades after, Young claims that the changes in the ear-lier time were greater than anything seen since (remember that the subsequent thirty years included the Great War!): 'I am speaking of changes in men's minds, and I cannot in my own time observe anything of greater consequence than the dethronement of ancient faith by natu-ral science and historical criticism and the transition from oligarchic to democratic representation.'[48]

The 1960s

Callum Brown has argued that the 1960s mark a pivotal period in the decline of Christianity in Britain, and attributes this to social and cultural changes then, particularly the changing status of women.[49] Crockett and Voas have argued that this claim that the 1960s were pivotal cannot be substantiated, for statistics show that religious decline has been gradual all through the twentieth century, generation by generation.[50] (In their evidence for general religious decline, they purport to include belief with adherence and attendance, but, as remarked above, the questions providing the data for belief are wildly non-specific and non-revealing.) Bruce and Glendenning have joined the fray, arguing that the long-term gradual decline holds up, but there is also some evidence for a 'moderate' form of the Brown thesis. They argue that much of the decline of the churches is explained not by adult defection but by a failure to keep children in the faith, and the decline in the 1960s could well lie in the experiences of the previous generation, notably the disruptive effects of total mobilisation for the Second World War (increasing participation of women in the labour market, greater mixing of men from different backgrounds in the services, large-scale re-housing), which disrupted traditional community and family ties and allowed young people to meet quite 'different others' on equal terms. From the war years onwards, young people increasingly married without regard to religion and then transmitted the 'disease of weak commitment' to their children.[51]

McLeod effectively agrees with a 'moderate form' of the Brown thesis (though disagreeing with many of Brown's specifics). In his study of precisely these years, *The Religious Crisis of the 1960s*, he concentrates on the 1960s but gives consideration both to influences from the remoter past and to subsequent developments. His focus is primarily the changing social, cultural, even legal status of Christianity, a 'quasi-Christendom' previously protected by laws relating to morality and religion like those prohibiting blasphemy, obscenity, suicide and homosexuality, those prescribing Sunday observance, censoring the media, and restricting gambling and drinking and abortion. McLeod makes no attempt to explain what he means by religion; and actually claims, as noted earlier, that secularisation theory depends on 'an artificially narrow definition of religion'.[52] But some clarity here would be helpful.[53] He completely misses my principal concern, the *new consciousness* which has come to distinguish the West. It is one thing to give the statistics for baptisms; it is another thing to draw attention to the different understanding of baptism (no longer a religious rite erasing original sin but a social rite of passage).[54]

I will argue here that, in the matter of belief, the 1960s were significant in many important ways. This is evident from the course of twentieth-century Protestant theology. The dominant liberal theology of the last decades of the nineteenth century had begun to take its bearings from the increasingly autonomous secular world. However, this trajectory petered out when liberal theology collapsed in the trauma of the First World War, and after the war Barth's neo-orthodoxy flourished, a counter-movement supposedly rooted in biblical data. But after the Second World War, with three decades of post-war boom, never equalled before or since, the secular world regained its 'attractiveness' and again became the arbiter of Christian theology: hence Bultmann in Germany and Tillich in the US. It was John Robinson's 1963 *Honest to God* that popularised this secularised theology, after which the trajectory was taken further by 'Death of God' theologians: Thomas J.J. Altizer's *The Gospel of Christian Atheism* (1966); Gabriel Vahanian's *The Death of God* (1961), Paul van Buren's *The Secular Meaning of the Gospel* (1966), Ronald Gregor Smith's *Secular Christianity* (1966) and even Harvey Cox's 1965 *Secular City*, which became a sort of manifesto for this new attitude towards the secular world. In both academic and popular theology it was the surrounding secular world that became the determining influence. Christianity became subjectivised in two senses. It lost its *out there* reality, and its frame of reference became intra-consciousness, all in the name of being relevant to the modern world.[55] Far from providing ground-breaking original insight, theology like Robinson's was completely reactive, taking its bearings from the ambient secular culture.[56]

These theologians' interlocutors were effectively their secular peers. This was the dynamic becoming increasingly evident throughout the 1960s.[57] David Lodge has bluntly remarked, 'Some time in the 1960s hell disappeared.'[58] And it took an entire metaphysic with it.

The dynamic so evident within Protestant theology is well illustrated within Catholicism (archetypically so) by the Second Vatican

Council (1962–65). This event can be interpreted in different ways, and the official Catholic line is that of 'continuity not rupture', and such a view can be justified from the council's documents, all of them the result of compromise. But a good deal of the official interpretation is so much spin. The Second Vatican Council is often hailed as the 'opening of the windows' of the Catholic Church. But in many ways this confuses cause and effect. Wilfred Sheed has written: 'He [John XXIII] wasn't opening any new windows: these had already been blown out one by one. He was accommodating to the wind.'[59]

O'Malley's fine study of the Second Vatican Council makes much of the three 'issues under the issues', namely the notion of change within Catholicism, the relation of centre to periphery, and the matter of style (or 'spirit').[60] But the biggest issue under the issues is hardly mentioned; namely, the eclipse of an otherworldly consciousness in the West. As I have argued, a new way of knowing had emerged, influenced by the scientific and technological revolutions; in line with this, a whole new way of experiencing reality emerged. O'Malley occasionally hints at the influence of 'the world',[61] though he restricts this to the political events after the Second World War.[62] He persists in finding the seeds of the Second Vatican Council in Catholic intellectuals like Lamennais, Guéranger, Migne or Lagrange, or in a liturgical or biblical encyclical of Pius XII, or in Catholic action, or in a return to the Fathers of the church.[63] But it is misleading to suggest that Vatican II was the germination of seeds planted by the likes of Lamennais; the modern world had changed everything, and Lamennais was merely conceding some aspects of this.

Normative authorities in the past, it is implied, had it all and we must return to them (by applying the 'proper hermeneutic') to recover the truth. In this reverence for past authorities, religion is of course not much different from other areas of human endeavour (medicine was returning to Galen right up till the eighteenth century), but this is precisely what modernity has changed. The form of knowledge associated with science does not depend on previous authorities; it is based on seeking something new through observation, testing novel hypotheses or devising novel experiments. The Second Vatican Council provides a classic illustration of the issue, the Decree on Religious Liberty (*Dignitatis humanae*).[64] 'Religious liberty' is the total opposite of what the Catholic Church had previously taught. Nevertheless, by the 1960s, the 'rightness' of religious liberty was so evident that it could not be resisted and was obviously what any body of responsible leaders would have to say. Attempts to justify this from the Catholic tradition involve enormous somersaulting and cherry-picking of amenable texts. This is no doubt why Cardinal Ritter of St Louis argued that the arguments should be dropped from the document, which should be limited to the simple affirmation and advocacy of religious liberty.[65]

The emphasis at the Second Vatican Council on 'the signs of the times' can be understood as accepting that Catholicism in the twentieth century must be in tune with the context—far from the magisterium expounding revelation 'once and for all delivered to the saints' (Jude 3). Talk of a 'hierarchy of truths' can be understood as a way of downgrading, without explicitly jettisoning, 'truths' no longer convincing. The priority of conscience is another way of secularising traditional Christianity: if, as was previously accepted, God has revealed his will and demands adherence to it, the fact that complying might cause difficulties is scarcely relevant.

The 1960s did see the culmination of a trend of Catholicism's capitulation to the surrounding culture. The Anti-Modernist Oath hitherto required of all clergy, the Index of Forbidden Books, minor orders and tonsure (abolished 1972), a congregation to guard what it deemed the legacy of the Council of Trent (abolished 1966),[66] were all discarded. Although they did not claim to be exhaustive worldviews (in the way, for example, that Thomism did), in the 1960s other 'this-worldly and activist theologies' moved in to fill at least some of the void: liberation theology, Black theology, feminist theology.[67]

The Protestant churches were no less affected, nowhere more evident than at the Fourth Assembly of the World Council of Churches (by then comprising 235 churches) held in Uppsala in 1968 with the theme 'Behold, I make all things new'. The General Secretary in his report for the Assembly felt it necessary to begin with a lengthy rebuttal of the criticism that 'the WCC is, by its involvement in social, economic and political questions, leading the churches away from their central task of proclaiming the Gospel, worshipping God and offering eternal salvation to a dying and sinful humanity'. No, he insisted, such this-worldly activity 'has always been the proper business of the Church'. 'This emphasis on man is not a turning away from God but a turning towards the God who most fully revealed himself in Jesus Christ.'[68] The Assembly's this-worldly orientation is overwhelmingly evident in the reports that each of the 'six sections' produced for general approval: not just (as might be expected) the sections on 'World Economic and Social Development', 'Towards Justice and Peace in International Affairs' and 'Towards New Styles of Living', but in what might be considered the more 'spiritual' sections.[69] The section on 'The Holy Spirit and the Catholicity of the Church' was split into one faction insisting on 'Christian solidarity with mankind' and a predominantly Orthodox faction which stressed the Christian unity given by and in Christ. The division was so profound that it gave rise to the possibility of a separate 'Orthodox minority report' or even none at all. One prominent participant, asked to provide a 'personal comment' on this section for the official record, observed: 'The discussion illustrated (not for the first time) how much nearer in some respects the Christians of the West (whether Roman, Anglican or Protestant) are to one another than to their brothers of the Orthodox East.'[70] Similarly the draft for the section on Worship drew opposition from a group (again predominantly Orthodox) objecting to the draft's 'secularising trend', or its 'assumption that *only* a world-centered and world-oriented Christianity is possible and permissible for Christians today'. Again the divergence was so great that it seemed no agreement could be reached, but a compromise eventuated advocating a 'cautious blessing' on the '"positive" forms of secularization'.[71] The editor of the Assembly's *Official Report* summed up:

> The most obvious and widely acknowledged feature of the Assembly was its preoccupation—at times, almost, its obsession—with the revolutionary ferment of our time, with questions of social and international responsibility, of war and peace and economic justice, with the pressing, agonizing physical needs of men, with the plight of the under-privileged, the homeless and starving, and with the most radical contemporary rebellions against all "establishments", civil and religious. It was not only recognized that—as it was often expressed—the world was writing the agenda for the meeting; the right of the world to do this was largely taken for granted.[72]

In this shift, the running has all been made by the surrounding culture. Consider, to return to Catholicism, the matter of indulgences.

Indulgences are a mechanism for remitting penance due to sin. General indulgences, offered to anyone prepared to fulfil the stipulated conditions, appeared in the eleventh century, and the first plenary indulgence (remission of all penance) was offered to participants in the first crusade (AD 1095). They became increasingly associated with pilgrimages, particularly the jubilee pilgrimage to Rome. In 1343 Pope Clement, in announcing a jubilee of 1350, formulated the full theory of indulgences, that Christ, along with Mary and the saints, had built up an inexhaustible 'Treasury of Merit' which anyone could draw on—and (a dubious refinement) draw on by contributing money. As is well known, the farming of indulgences became the trigger of the Reformation. As late as 1967 Pope Paul VI defended this general teaching in his apostolic constitution *Indulgentiarum doctrina*. Yet when the pope had floated this document at the Second Vatican Council it had received a savaging from nearly all permitted to comment.[73] True, the Apostolic Penitentiary announced that a plenary indulgence would be granted to all who 'devoutly participate' in the Ninth World Meeting of Families in Dublin in August 2018, and Archbishop Eamon Martin of Armagh urged people not to look to the indulgence for personal benefit, but for the benefit of 'a relative or friend who has gone to their rest who may be in need of God's mercy'.[74] Nevertheless, a general shift of understanding has made indulgences difficult to comprehend, part of a bygone mindset, effectively a dead letter.

A similar fate has befallen relics. In the Middle Ages, 'The cult of the saints was at the very heart of popular religion. Luchaire did not exaggerate when he wrote that "the true religion of the middle age, to be frank, is the worship of relics".'[75] Relics have now become more an embarrassment than an object of devotion. Even the relics in the Roman basilica of Santa Croce in Gerusalemme, the core being those St Helena brought back from the Holy Land in the fourth century (including two reputed thorns of the crown of thorns, a nail and three small fragments of the true cross), which even a few decades ago were prominently displayed, are now discreetly sidelined. A tourist who knows of their existence could find them, but any public display has disappeared.[76]

This shift away from the supernatural, from the strictly religious in the sense understood throughout this book, is evident everywhere. The entire sacramental principle was widely rethought. I mentioned above Lodge's remark that an entire metaphysic had disappeared. This supernatural metaphysic had underpinned the entire sacramental system, which came to be hollowed out and receded to the periphery (though not officially repudiated). It was in the 1960s that ordinary Catholics simply ceased to 'go to confession' to be absolved from sins threatening eternal punishment. The sacrament of 'confession' was reconceptualised as 'reconciliation'.[77] Extreme unction, which a few centuries before instilled dread,[78] likewise needed to be reconceptualised as the 'sacrament of the sick', because the idea of eternal life being conferred (or eternal punishment avoided) through an anointing with oil ceased to carry force. Stark is incorrect when he attributes declining mass attendance afterwards to a directive of the Vatican Council that 'it was no longer a sin to miss Mass'.[79] There was no such directive; Catholics just decided for themselves. Practices like benediction or adoration of the Blessed Sacrament and Eucharistic processions simply failed to carry their traditional appeal, and the Eucharist, for centuries understood as 'the real presence' (explained officially through transubstantiation), was reconceptualised in concepts like 'trans-signification'. In her biography of Luther (a believer in transubstantiation all his life), Roper writes: 'In Wittenberg in 1543, when some communion wine was spilled on a woman's jacket and the back of her pew, he and Bugenhagen [the organiser of Lutheranism in northern Germany and Scandinavia] not only licked it off her coat but went so far as to cut out the bits of the jacket they had been unable to clean, plane away the sections of her pew where the wine had splashed, and burn the lot'.[80] This may seem excessive, but not if one believes in a hard sense that this is no longer wine but the blood of the second person of the Trinity. Up till the 1960s, in a case of spilled consecrated wine, Catholic rubrics required measures approximating to Luther's. But in the 1960s these were abolished, replaced by directives far more relaxed. I have heard the Anglican theologian Leslie Houlden suggest that these new regulations show that Catholics have effectively ceased to hold to the real presence.[81] In these and many other ways, the supernatural receded before the empirical. Many Catholics simply drifted away, but (my point here) even for many who continued to call themselves Catholic and to attend church, the rationale for the sacraments had changed.

Even when the form was preserved, the otherworldly reference had receded. This is the hollowing out of belief, even for those still understanding themselves as believers.

Around the 1960s, social activism became the order of the day, something in many cases motivated by recognisably traditional Christian belief, but not necessarily so. A good deal of this social involvement can be understood to corroborate the main theme of this book. The English playwright David Hare in 1993 produced a trilogy examining contemporary Britain through the institutions of the church, the law and politics. He records:

> Very early on in my researches into the Church of England, I was aston-
> ished to find a group of inner-city priests who had virtually abandoned
> their aim of bringing souls to Christ, but who were interpreting their
> religious mission as social work, pure and simple. Although I myself had
> been educated in a devout Christian school and was now moved to
> write a play which sought to restore to the stage the ancient subject of
> man's relationship with the gods, I found to my surprise that many
> good priests almost refused to discuss God with me. They had ceased
> to believe that the divine could, in any significant way, be separated
> from the social.[82]

Christianity can undoubtedly motivate social responsibility; it can also be reduced to it. In 1976, the Jesuit priest and renowned anti-war campaigner Daniel Berrigan wrote in a private letter responding to a query about Henry Thoreau's rejection of established religion:

> I think I've made a break with formal religion no less clean than
> Thoreau: I don't make an issue of it because there are more serious
> tasks than beating on the church, which but for its real estate and build-
> ings, is already dead on its cloven feet. As far as Christianity is con-
> cerned, I love the New Testament, and have some good friends who
> believe with that and who lay something out in consequence. I guess
> that's all one can reasonably expect these days. Indeed, maybe it was
> never much different than that.[83]

The emptying out of Christianity to become social involvement is well attested.[84]

As secularisation theorists record, the numbers attending Sunday schools plummeted, but a more important change was the nature of what was taught. If until the 1960s books like Sheehan's *Apologetics and*

Christian Doctrine were standard fare for Catholics, they were subtly displaced by a different content altogether. 'A typical religious education textbook from the post-Vatican II period wouldn't deny basic Christian teachings like the Resurrection and the Atonement, or specifically Catholic concepts like purgatory and the intercession of the saints—but it would often ignore or minimize them, substituting the language of self-actualization and personal growth, until it became hard to distinguish a religious education manual from a typical handbook for building self-esteem.'[85]

That the 1960s saw this internal secularisation gather momentum is probably due to many factors. We have already referred to the generational delay of the effects of total mobilisation for the Second World War, which had broken down previous barriers to marriage beyond one's own community; this made passing on a distinct religious tradition problematic. The post-war affluence has been mentioned. The effect of affluence is to loosen ties to community, or to encourage individualism. Above all, however, looms education. Chadwick has written: 'The nineteenth century turned vast illiterate Catholic populations into half-literate Catholic populations. The first half of the twentieth century turned half-literate Catholic populations into an almost entirely literate people.'[86] This applies more widely than to Catholics. All these factors (affluence, individualism, education) affect the West primarily, reinforcing the divide between the West and elsewhere.

Internal secularisation

This shift, of course, has not gone uncontested. Popes John Paul II and Benedict XVI can be understood as not only upholding traditional teachings but also insisting on the metaphysic underpinning them. Cardinal Ratzinger often railed against 'secularism ... presented as an ideology ... as if it were the only voice of rationality, when it is only the expression of a "certain rationalism"'.[87] The Ratzinger *Catechism of the Catholic Church* (1992) is a response to the 'content-lite' catechetics courses mentioned above (as well, of course, to the liberal *Dutch Catechism* of 1966). By contrast, the acclaim given Pope Francis's encyclical *Laudato si'* can be understood in the way suggested here. Of course, he undoubtedly sees (and would loudly assert that he sees) that his concern with the environment stems from his understanding of God's demands, and many others undoubtedly share the same supernatural motivation. But the point is that a concern with the environment does not depend in any exclusive sense on any supernatural awareness, nor does the concern for refugees, migration, economic inequality, the abuses of unfettered capitalism and other issues for which he has drawn accolades.[88]

Catholic intellectuals have been equally caught up in this cognitive shift. Thomas Sheehan began a long controversy with his 1984 article 'Revolution in the Church' in the *New York Review of Books*. This was a review of the German theologian Hans Küng's *Eternal Life?* which effectively reinterpreted (or hollowed out) the traditional ideas of the resurrection of Jesus and human immortality. In his review Sheehan spoke of the 'liberal consensus' of Catholic scholars which (he claimed) denied among other things Jesus' messianic claims, his miracles, his intention to found a church.[89] Michael Dummett, Wykeham Professor of Logic at Oxford and a Catholic, protested that this 'liberal consensus' fundamentally conflicted with any traditional Catholic understanding of the faith and reduced the church to a fraud.[90] In a subsequent contribution to the debate, Dummett insisted: 'If these views [of the "liberal consensus"] are to be regarded as consistent with the church's teaching, then that teaching is reduced to a demand for the acceptance of certain forms of words, which may be taken as expressing anything one chooses.'[91]

Rethinking the idea of an afterlife extends well beyond Catholicism. In another novel David Lodge has remarked:

> The concepts and images of this next world which have come down to us in Christian teaching no longer have any credibility for thoughtful, educated men and women. The very idea of an afterlife for individual human beings has been regarded with skepticism and embarrassment— or silently ignored—by nearly every major twentieth-century theologian. Bultmann, Barth, Bonhoeffer, Tillich, for example, even the Jesuit Karl Rahner, all dismissed traditional notions of personal survival after death ... Rahner said in an interview, "with death it's all over. Life is past and it won't come again". In print he was more circumspect, arguing that the soul would survive, but in a non-personal "pancosmic" state ... This however is mere metaphysical doodling.[92]

All mainline denominations have seemingly become homogenised into repeating high-minded humanism, even if peppered with biblical references. The renowned Lutheran theologian Carl Braaten wrote to Mark Hanson, presiding Bishop of the Evangelical Lutheran Church of America, bemoaning what had become of his tradition:

> The kind of Lutheranism that I learned—from Nygren, Aulen, Bring, Pinomaa, Schlink, P. Brunner, Bonhoeffer, Pannenberg, Piepkorn, Quanbeck, Preus, and Lindbeck, not to mention the pious missionary teachers from whom I learned the Bible, the Catechism, and the Christian faith—and taught in a Lutheran parish and seminary for many years is now marginalised to the point of near extinction. In looking for evidence that could convincingly contradict the charge that the ELCA has become just another liberal Protestant denomination, it would seem reasonable to examine what is produced by its publishing house, theological schools, magazine publications, church council resolutions, commission statements, task force recommendations, statements and actions by its bishops. The end result is an embarrassment ... I must tell you that I read all your episcopal letters that come across my desk. But I must also tell you that your stated convictions, punctuated by many pious sentiments, are not significantly distinguishable from those that come from the liberal Protestant leaders of other American denominations.[93]

For Anglicans, consider Nick Spencer's *A Future for Christianity*, with its foreword provided by both the Archbishop of Canterbury and the Cardinal Archbishop of Westminster. Although Spencer never misses an opportunity to repeat conventional wisdom denying the secularisation thesis, he effectively admits it here: 'The common Christian culture into which virtually every English, Scottish, Welsh and Northern/Irish person has been born for the last millennium is passing, to be replaced by a confusing plural patchwork, haunted by strong Christian associations.'[94] He makes no effort to show that this contemporary 'lively, fermenting, complex storm of spiritual ideas, practices and commitments' is religious in the substantive sense which has been characteristic of Western Christianity.[95] Spencer is convinced that Christianity has a 'future', but the future that he envisages is one of social involvement. He labels this 'social liturgy' to distinguish it from the 'social gospel' of the early part of the twentieth century in the US, which came to lose the 'gospel' dimension and become mere social activism. However,

Spencer's insistence that Christians must hold fast to the gospel does not show how his social liturgy will avoid going the way of the social gospel. Arguing that persistence, relationality and localised engagement, and qualities like an emphasis on hospitality, hopefulness and unconditional acceptance, will show the 'authentically Christian nature' of 'social liturgy' goes a long way towards conceding the internal secularisation of Christianity.[96] His final sentences, that this social liturgy would perhaps 'bring the life of churches close to that of the earliest church—[in its] forgiveness, generosity and love', underplay the dynamic operative in the early church.[97] The first Christians could display forgiveness, generosity and love because of what they considered their personal experience of God's saving activity; but forgiveness, generosity and love have no need to be based on such an experience, and many in the modern world have dispensed with it.

The above examples illustrate the effects of the cognitive shift characterising modern Western culture, or what I have called the peripheralising of the otherworldly. This has struck at the very rationale underlying traditional religion in the West—unless one argues for 'American exceptionalism'.

4

US EXCEPTIONALISM

Bruce begins a study of just this issue with a rather mischievous sentence: 'If we leave aside the social, moral and political behaviour of its citizens, the United States has every appearance of being unusually godly.'[1] It seems widely accepted in the contemporary academic field of religion that although Europe may be secularised, the US is not. Hence, it is claimed, we have 'Religious America' in contrast to 'Secular Europe'.[2] Thus, many go on to add, the secularisation thesis falls because the US, the most modern nation of all, remains profoundly religious.

But this is where precision is crucial. Addressing precisely this question of the religious divide between America and Europe, Howard begins by noting two different understandings of the term religion: one denotes belief and activity relating to a higher realm, the other denotes issues arising from and activities performed in connection with denominational affiliation.[3] His book deals almost exclusively with the latter. Why Americans perform so much voluntary activity under the label of Christianity while Europeans do far less is an interesting question; but it is a very different question from whether or not Americans have preserved a sense of the supernatural that Europeans have lost, which is often insinuated on the strength of Americans' constant invocation of Christianity.

'Religion' in the US undoubtedly has to fulfil so many more roles than simply relating to entities of another order—social, political and cultural roles. Berger himself admits this when he tells of a colleague who had grown up a Baptist, but who, having become a professor, joined a Methodist church. Berger writes: 'I already had some sense of the denominational status system, so I asked him: "Why not Episcopalian?" He replied: "No, that would be pushing it."'[4] Berger is here flagging up a significant difference from Europe, where becoming a professor typically entails no religious considerations of any kind. It hardly proves, though, that the US is more religious in any substantive sense.

Woodward considers that 'Americans, even now, can simultaneously be both pervasively secular and persistently religious—still a puzzle to Europeans'.[5] No, it is not a puzzle; Americans can be pervasively secular according to Howard's first meaning of the word religion, persistently religious in his second.

Evangelical revival

Berger gave, as two of his reasons for recanting the secularisation thesis, the counterculture and the Evangelical revival. We have already dealt with the counterculture in dealing with the New Age. We can simply repeat that if words like 'the divine' and 'the transcendent within' are understood in a strict sense, of course you have religion as understood in this book. But if these terms refer only to discovering one's 'essential *isness*' and achieving harmony with the universe, you have something else altogether—laudable perhaps, and no doubt helpful for many, but confirming rather than disproving the secularisation thesis.

Even more than the counterculture, it is the Evangelical revival that has attracted recent attention. There was always a strain of American Christianity which reacted against the liberalisation of the mainline denominations, once German biblical criticism and Darwinism reached America (their advent and impact were delayed because of the Civil War and its aftermath). This Christianity, under the banner of biblical inerrancy, came to be called fundamentalist. Some still glory in this label. There are Creation museums in many states, and occasionally state school boards pass laws outlawing Darwin 'in favour of the Bible'.[6] America's biggest Protestant denomination, the Southern Baptist Convention, came to be taken over by this faction beginning in the 1970s, a process complete by 1990.[7] Again, recalling Wilson's comment that 'this pious biblicism appears to have no impact whatsoever on the assumptions on which the social system operates', one might ask whether this strident claim for biblical inerrancy is a genuine hermeneutic tool or a signifier for something else.[8]

If some have maintained the 'fundamentalist' label, most in this sector moved, beginning in the 1950s, to a less confrontational approach labelled Evangelical, personified by Billy Graham (1918–2018), whose global profile (he is reputed to have preached to 215 million people in 185 countries) established him as *the* face of American Christianity.[9] In fact, his closeness to American Presidents and his Cold War anti-communism and pro-Vietnam War stance established him for many as the face of *America*. In that political role, we catch another glimpse of the different elements in America's complex mix often labelled simply 'religion'. Indeed, a former President of Britain's Methodist Conference in his sharply critical review of Graham's ('grandly misnamed') autobiography, *Just as I Am*, reduced Graham's message to 'just an invitation to "take Jesus into your heart" and a solidarity with the values of the American dream'.[10]

This Evangelical sector came to prominence in the 1970s with its politicisation and the 'Moral Majority', personified in Jerry Falwell with his 'holy war' against 'secular humanism'. Wuthnow has well shown how the category of 'born again' gained prominence in 1976, when presidential candidate Jimmy Carter claimed to be 'Evangelical' and 'born again'—to the perplexity of liberal media pundits. Polls were required to establish what this rather unfamiliar category of Christian signified, how many there were—and whom they would vote for. There was enormous discrepancy, not least because different polls collected their data on quickly answerable and often differing questions. Their numbers were calculated to be anything between 8% and 40% of the population. And the political dimension was never far below the surface. 'The standard polling question ask[ed] pollees to respond yes or no with regard to having been "born again" ... The reason the question persists in polls is because it provides a crude indication of the likelihood that someone will vote Republican or support some political issue such as legislation against abortion or same-sex marriage.'[11] This is the significance of Wuthnow's title: *Inventing American Religion*. It is this political concern that, although not creating the category, has given it its prominence.

The fact that this 'religious right' was the conscious creation of Richard Viguerie, Paul Weyrich and Howard Phillips, two Catholics and a Jew, who realised that the mailing lists of televangelists could be mobilised as a political resource, is itself revealing. This raises the question whether we are dealing with something religious or political, a question that a substantive view of religion helps address. During these years America's political scene was becoming polarised. The Democratic Party became increasingly associated with identity politics, home for African Americans, feminists, gays and the pro-choice lobby. The Republicans presented themselves as maintaining traditional values, the family and the 'pro-life' movement. Over time, this split became almost complete in America's 'culture wars', with particularly the issue of abortion becoming the distinguishing mark, almost a litmus test.

The element of race cannot be left out of this analysis. Posner argues that it is a myth that it was the 1973 *Roe* v *Wade* decision of the Supreme Court that motivated Evangelicals to rise up to protect 'the unborn'. As Moral Majority co-founder Paul Weyrich has acknowledged, 'the movement was actually galvanized in the 1970s and early 1980s when the IRS revoked the tax-exempt status of Bob Jones University and other conservative Christian schools that refused to accept nonwhites'. It was the government's actions against segregation and 'Southern values' that triggered the rise of the Evangelicals. Posner cites Randall Balmer, a respected historian of American religion: 'The overwhelming support for Trump heralds the religious right coming full circle to embrace its roots in racism. The breakthrough of the 2016 election lies in the fact that the religious right, in its support for a thrice-married, self-confessed sexual predator, finally dispensed with the fiction that it was concerned about abortion or "family values".'[12] One does not have to see this as an adequate, much less a complete, explanation, but it does highlight the 'non-religious' aspects of what is often taken at its own evaluation as a professedly 'religious' movement.

The origins of 'Evangelicalism' in the Puritan heritage are obvious. However, although for all sorts of reasons such a movement may tout its Christian credentials, this may not necessarily be the most helpful way to understand it. Evangelical Christianity in the US may in many ways be explicable as a cultural and political reaction against the liberal consensus of the east and west coasts—against the present shape of the

Democratic Party. The element of reaction *may* involve concern with the deity, and a renewed appropriation of profoundly Christian ideas like divine sovereignty, predestination, particular providence, human depravity and so on, but the presumption that this is necessarily the case is unwarranted. The fact that Donald Trump won 81 per cent of the white Evangelical vote, a higher percentage than George W. Bush, John McCain or Mitt Romney, has drawn attention to the socio-polit-ico-cultural element within 'Evangelicalism'.[13]

The culture wars so associated with Evangelicals have affected other denominations, most notably Catholics; indeed, the 'religious right' is commonly said to comprise Evangelicals and Catholics. As noted, US political parties have polarised into 'pro-choice' (Democrats) and 'pro-life' (Republicans). US Catholic bishops, nearly all appointed during the long reign of Pope John Paul II, who in his 1995 encyclical *Evangelium vitae* had declared with full papal authority that human life begins at the moment of conception, have generally seemed to make abortion the *sine qua non* of Catholicism, in opposition to those like Chicago's Cardinal Bernardin who argued for a 'consistent ethic of life', embracing genetics, abortion, capital punishment, modern warfare and care of the terminally ill. This became anything but a discreet Catholic matter when bishops threatened to excommunicate or deny communion to politicians who were not prepared to outlaw abortion in any guise.[14] There is a vocal sector of American Catholicism that promotes this single-minded focus. George Weigel, best known for his adulatory biography of John Paul II, writes: 'An unambiguous, indeed happily robust, pro-life position, embodied in action and not just in abstract declarations of adhesion to Catholic teaching, is now *the* cultural marker of seriousness about Catholic identity in the American public square.'[15] In the polarised American political scene, this is joining the culture wars.

However, Steinfels well shows that those identifying as Catholics have a much more nuanced position than the hierarchy. Wording in polls is (as noted on several occasions above) crucial; however, in a 2000 'American Catholics in the Public Square' study, when asked 'If you had to choose, would you describe yourself as more pro-life or more pro-choice', self-identified Catholics were almost equally divided, with 46% opting for pro-life, 49% for pro-choice, and 5%

unable or unwilling to respond.[16] It is the hierarchy, especially the 'culture warriors' among them, that have given this issue its artificially high priority, which has been called into question by the more nuanced approach of Pope Francis attempting to transcend these culture wars.

Capitalism

There is a remarkable American Catholic phenomenon of 'reinterpreting' papal statements for the American public. Conservatives behind the journal *First Things* (Weigel prominent among them) went out of their way to promote the 1991 encyclical *Centesimus annus*, the first papal encyclical after the fall of communism, as a vindication of their own pro-capitalist agenda. By some hours, they pre-empted publication of the encyclical in Rome with Richard John Neuhaus's *Wall Street Journal* article under the heading 'Pope Affirms the "New Capitalism"'. As one commentator observed, 'The column portrayed the encyclical as "a ringing endorsement of the market economy", claimed that its central message was that "capitalism is the economic corollary of the Christian understanding of man's nature and destiny", and chided left-wing American bishops for being out of step with "the Church's authoritative teaching".' The next day Weigel promoted the same views in the *Los Angeles Times*.[17]

Another pro-American-capitalism Catholic, Michael Novak, had already done the same for the 1987 encyclical *Sollicitudo rei socialis*, which had branded both liberal capitalism and Marxist collectivism as 'imperfect and in need of radical correction'. Novak noted the 'dismay among Americans' at what on the face of it seemed like 'moral equivalence' between capitalism and socialism. He admitted that the Pope was 'vulnerable to criticism for the unguarded way' he drew parallels. But, argued Novak, a close reading of the text showed that this was not the Pope's real view. Certainly Pope John Paul continued to voice criticisms found in Paul VI's 1967 'too optimistic' encyclical *Populorum progressio*, whose twentieth anniversary *Sollicitudo rei socialis* was marking, but his picture of 'liberal capitalism ... presents a caricature'. Nevertheless, criticism of the encyclical is actually unjustified because if one looks carefully at the underlying 'theological vision', one clearly sees it is based on global solidarity, an essential prerequisite of which 'is autonomy and free self-determination', for which democracy is 'the necessary condition'. So, 'according to the encyclical's stated prescriptions, the world the Pope desires would have in structure something very much like the institutions of the United States'. While there is 'no excuse for the few careless passages on parallelism between East and West', by 'focusing on the theological vision ... there is much to take strength from'.[18]

Such reinterpretation was given a novel slant by George Weigel in his reaction to Benedict XVI's 2009 encyclical *Caritas in veritate*, which united spirituality and social involvement in the concept of 'integral human development'. The Pope deplored the 'financialisation' of life itself, and (among other things) called for some overall supervisory agency for the global economy and protection of the environment. Weigel called the encyclical a 'duck-billed platypus' (an allusion to that animal's seeming combination of incompatible elements). One could go through it, claimed Weigel, and highlight with a gold marker the ideas coming genuinely from the Pope, and with a red marker the ideas coming from elsewhere.[19] Weigel spelt this out further in an article for *Polska* daily, titled 'Capitalism Is the Only Catholic System', excerpts of which were published by Poland's church-run Catholic Information Agency. He called the encyclical a 'complicated and in places unclear document', shaped by 'incoherent sentimentalism', constituting 'a kind of hybrid' of the Pope's true beliefs and 'plots and demands of intellectuals and activists'. 'There are fragments of *Caritas in Veritate*, easily recognizable to people who know the mentality and thinking of Joseph Ratzinger, which develop the line of John Paul II ... The trouble is with those fragments which seem to reflect the convictions of the Pontifical Council for Justice and Peace, and which show distinct left-wing leanings like similar bodies in other Christian and ecumenical communities.'[20]

Weigel similarly interpreted Pope Francis's encyclical on the environment, *Laudato si'*. 'If you read the encyclical as "the global-warming encyclical", you will miss the heart and soul of what this sprawling encyclical is about.' The Pope states explicitly that 'the Church does not presume to settle scientific questions or to replace politics'. Weigel urges us to approach the document as 'religious and cultural'. The document speaks 'to the flaws in humanity's understanding of itself today [and points us] in a more noble direction'. Again, the theological vision underneath is the essential thing: it is 'an encyclical primarily about *us*, and not primarily about trees, plankton and the Tennessee snail darter'.[21]

These opinion pieces, as intended, set the tone for much of the coverage of these encyclicals in the American media. This relentless insistence on 'clarifying' Catholic statements according to a political agenda seems a uniquely American phenomenon, and brings to mind nothing so much as Herberg's observation: 'By every realistic criterion, the American Way of Life is the operative faith of the American people.'[22] Again, one can profitably try to differentiate the religious from the political.

In his fine study *Capitalism and Christianity, American Style*, Connolly shows their fusion in all its complexity. There is, says Connolly, no pure form of realities like capitalism and Christianity. There is a 'capitalist axiomatic', 'a set of elements knotted together in a way that resists capture by a formal analysis'. Christianity is just as complex a reality. Christianity 'is both a long-term shifting constellation of existential experiments and a set of contending spiritual dispositions'.[23] In any particular 'state-capital-Christian complex', all these diverse elements are imbricated, intercalated, infused, incorporated (words Connolly likes) in their own special way. Seeking to identify particular elements as causes is complex because state-capital-Christian imbrications preclude attempts to separate out any one component autonomously. Each interacts with the several others, and in that interaction all are liable to change. 'Causality, as relations of dependence between separate factors, morphs into energized complexities of mutual imbrication and inter-involvement, in which heretofore unconnected or loosely associated elements—*fold, bend, blend, emulsify and resolve incompletely into each other*—forging a qualitative assemblage resistant to classical models of explanation.'[24] In this way Connolly explains the messy links between capitalism and Christianity in contemporary America: they combine in an 'evangelical-capitalist resonance machine'.[25] Connolly understands Christianity more as 'Christian tradition' than 'Christian religion' in our sense, but his study helpfully shows that, although completely separating out components in this mix may be impossible, we can at least be aware of the mix and the purposes it serves. Components may be mixed in very unequal quantities. Attempting the difficult differentiation is worth the effort.

Prosperity gospel

Even serious scholars like Casanova can glibly talk of 'American religious vitality'.[26] But many such scholars seem to have little interest in what this religion actually consists of. The American dream always promised success, prosperity and upward mobility, achieved through application and hard work, in a society offering little in the way of obstruction or hindrance. One form of this ideal was given a particular philosophical underpinning by Herbert Spencer (1820–1903) who justified the social ascent of the privileged classes. It was he, not Darwin, who coined the phrase 'survival of the fittest', and in reference to economic and political life, not the animal world. His thinking was much more influential in America than Britain[27] because never before in any country had so many been so rich or enjoyed their wealth so much.

> In consequence of Spencer no-one needed to feel the slightest guilt over this good fortune. It was the inevitable result of natural strength, inherent capacity to adapt … The ideas also protected wealth. No one, and especially no government, could touch it or the methods by which it was acquired or was being enlarged. To do so would interfere with the desperately essential process by which the race was being improved. It might seem a problem for the rich that so many were so poor … But Herbert Spencer took care of this embarrassment as well. To help the poor, either by private or public aid, also interfered disastrously with the improvement of the race.[28]

Spencer's ideas fitted perfectly the needs of the time, answering almost miraculously the needs of America's wealthy classes.[29] John D. Rockefeller declared in a Sunday school address: 'The growth of a large business is merely a survival of the fittest … The American Beauty rose can be produced in the splendor and fragrance which bring cheer to its beholder only by sacrificing the early buds which grow up around it. This is not an evil tendency in business. It is merely the working out of a law of nature and a law of God.'[30] And Andrew Carnegie, a complete Spencerian, could state: 'We accept and welcome, therefore, as conditions to which we must accommodate ourselves, great inequality of environment; the concentration of business, industrial and commercial, in the hands of a few; and the law of competition between these, as being not only beneficial, but essential to the future progress of the race.'[31] Wealth is nothing to be guilty about. To quote Rockefeller again: 'I believe the power to make money is a gift of God. It is my duty to make money and still more money, and to use the money I make for the good of my fellow man according to the dictates of my conscience.'[32]

This Spencerian thinking had a profound influence on churches. Many church leaders and theologians looked with favour and enthusiasm on the American system of acquisition and enjoyment, and pronounced it socially and morally above reproach. Famous Spencerian churchmen like Henry Ward Beecher and De Witt Talmage actually expressed disdain for the working classes.[33] Episcopal Bishop William Lawrence stated: 'It is only to the man of morality that wealth comes ... Godliness is in league with riches.'[34] Perhaps the most notorious exponent of these views was Russell H. Conwell, from 1879 pastor of Grace Baptist Church in Philadelphia and founder of Temple University. His 'Acres of Diamonds' sermon was delivered over five thousand times across America. In this he declared:

> Never in the history of the world did a poor man without capital have such an opportunity to get rich quickly and honestly as he does now in our city ... I say that you ought to get rich, and it is your duty to get rich ... To make money honestly is to preach the gospel ... The number of poor who are to be sympathized with is very small. To sympathize with a man whom God has punished for his sins, thus to help him when God would still continue a just punishment, is to do wrong, no doubt about it, and we do that more than we help those who are deserving. While we should sympathize with God's poor—that is, those who cannot help themselves—let us remember there is not a poor person in the United States who was not made poor by his own shortcomings, or by the shortcomings of someone else. It is all wrong to be poor anyhow.[35]

In the post-war years before the first OPEC price-hike in 1974, when the world led by America was undergoing a period of growth never experienced in recorded history, the American dream was recast for Everyman. Norman Vincent Peale, a Presbyterian (and at one time Donald Trump's pastor, and minister at Trump's first wedding), gave it a popular twist in *The Power of Positive Thinking*. His basic message was: this is the land of opportunity, so get out there and win through self-confidence and a positive mental attitude. 'Attitudes are more important than facts', he insisted;[36] thoughts create circumstances, not vice versa.[37] The Bible functions as a mine of positive thoughts: positive-thinking techniques often include reciting biblical texts, but the Bible is not unique here—Emerson, William James, Thoreau, and even Euripides, Socrates and Marcus Aurelius will do just as well. (So much for claims for the Bible's uniqueness within Peale's kind of Evangelicalism.) There is much about a higher power; this is deliberately left vague and Christians are quite free to understand this power as the Christian God, but this is not necessary. There is nothing about a spiritual guide being necessary (except perhaps a guide like Peale himself for purposes of motivation) in this expressly 'self-improvement process';[38] it is up to you to make your life a success.

There has been an identifiable mutation of this thinking giving rise to the 'prosperity gospel', which lays more stress on God's provision than individual entrepreneurial initiative (and today there are unlimited variations possible in balancing the two). God's provision often depended on tithes and offerings, 'faith' widely and quickly morphing into 'seed faith' or the 'plant-so-you-may-reap' idea, perhaps originating from A.A. Allen (1911–70). This form of the prosperity gospel came to be associated with names like Kenneth Hagin ('If you drive a mere Chevrolet and not a luxury car you have not understood the Gospel'[39]), Oral Roberts (God would 'call me home' unless followers donate $8 million), Jim and Tammy Faye Bakker of PTL Club and Heritage USA (with their 50-foot walk-in closets, gold-plated bathroom fixtures and air-conditioned dog kennels), and Kenneth and Gloria Copeland ('Give $1 for the sake of the Gospel and $100 belongs to you'[40]). Pentecostalism has a close structural link to this hucksterish prosperity gospel, as Douthat remarks: 'Pentecostalism's entrepreneurial structure, in which every church is effectively a start-up, has always attracted ministers prone to the kind of self-aggrandizement that's more easily justified by prosperity theology than by more orthodox strands of Christian faith.'[41]

Most today would positively repudiate the prosperity gospel, but such a repudiation may give rise to confusion because often it covers the prosperity gospel only in its most crass and self-enriching 'seed-faith' formulation, and is a ploy to distance the speaker from the hucksters, shysters and charlatans. Nevertheless, one informed observer calls the prosperity gospel a diffuse American Christian movement that links faith, positive thinking and material wealth into 'the American religion of winning ... There's something in the air in American religion that has valorized business success, wealth and "vigor".' He claims that perhaps close to two-thirds of Americans identify with at least some prosperity gospel teachings, 'such as the idea that God wants people to succeed financially'.[42] So many churches embody and encourage the American dream of victory and achievement, endowing wealth with respectability and equating success with virtue.[43]

Kate Bowler of Duke University claims that three of America's twelve largest churches (Joel Osteen's in Houston, Tommy Barnett's in Phoenix and T.D. Jakes' in Dallas) are prosperity churches. (In assessing her estimates, bear in mind that, as mentioned above, emphases on all-round success are found far more widely than in prosperity churches narrowly so called.) She claims that of America's second-tier churches—those with about 5,000 members—the prosperity gospel dominates. Overall, she estimates that 50 of the largest 260 churches in America preach prosperity, particularly in the Sun Belt of California, Florida and Arizona and among African Americans and Hispanics.[44] Above all, it is the financial ministries so obvious since the 1980s that clearly promote a message fitted to a society so valuing upward mobility. Consider the Texas evangelist Mike Murdock with his achievement message, can-do manuals and endless lists: *31 Secrets for Career Success*, *Secrets of the Richest Man Who Ever Lived: 31 Master Secrets from the Life of King Solomon*, and *31 Reaon People Do Not Receive Their Financial Harve$t*. His 'School of Financial Success' videos include titles like: 'Solomon's 17 Secrets for Achievement'; 'Paul's 26 Principles of Successful Negotiations'; '25 Steps to Abundance'; 'Seven Ways to Stay Motivated'; 'Five Keys to Achieving Goals'; and 'Ten Steps for Overcoming Financial Adversity'.

Murdock can be supremely crass in his prosperity preaching. But, to repeat: a recognisable form of the prosperity gospel is widely accepted. Kirbyjon Caldwell, a Methodist mega-pastor in Houston and author of *The Gospel of Good Success: A Road Map to Spiritual, Emotional, and Financial Wholeness*, gave the benediction at both of George W. Bush's inaugurals.[45] Paula White, one of the five church representatives speaking at Donald Trump's 2017 inaugural, is far more crass. She is known for calling for 'demon-slaying, abundance-bringing' donations of $229 to ensure all-round prosperity—in reference to 1 Chronicles 22.9, which describes Solomon's winning respite from 'enemies on every side'.[46]

Thus so many who may explicitly repudiate the 'gospel of prosperity' must nevertheless be considered as preaching success, victory, achievement in the capitalist system. Consider Joel Osteen of Houston's Lakeside Church, America's largest church with 38,000 members. His message is 'Press on and aim high', peppered with copious biblical references. Bowler remarks: 'Osteen is often derided as Christianity Lite, but he is more like Positivity Extreme.'[47] Collected sermons published include: *Your Best Life Now: Seven Steps to Living at Your Full Potential, Become a Better You: Seven Keys to Improving Your Life Every Day*, and *It's Your Time: Activate Your Faith, Achieve Your Dreams, and Increase in God's Favor*. It is not impossible that many of his congregation have some form of otherworldly Christianity strengthened; I mentioned above that the balance between divine provision and individual initiative can vary enormously. However, a supernatural element cannot be presumed. Osteen's publications could just as properly be classified in bookshops under 'Self-Help and Personal Growth' as under 'Religion'.[48]

Even Rick Warren of California's Saddleback mega-church with over 20,000 members, again expressly repudiating the prosperity gospel, is essentially preaching fulfilment in life. One admiring assessment of his 30-million seller *The Purpose Driven Life* notes: 'It is tempting to interpret the book's message as a kind of New Age self-help theology.' The assessment adds defensively: 'If the vision of faith sometimes seems skimpy, that's because the book is supposed to be supplemented by a layer of discussion and reflection and debate.'[49] (In parenthesis, I may add that Warren insists: 'I do believe the Bible is literally true. I believe the stories in it actually happened,'[50] but as one who has actually undergone his 'Purpose Driven Church' workshop, I can testify that little in that seminar was built on the Bible; he was introducing the organisational principles of Coca-Cola, Colgate, Microsoft, into the running of voluntary associations—another insight into Wilson's dictum: 'This pious biblicism appears to have no impact whatsoever on the assumptions on which the social system operates.')

America's churches are called on to perform so many functions besides relating to another reality. Americans, so many migratory

(10 per cent of the population have been said to move every year), need somewhere to find a home, to belong, to fit in. The guru of social capital, Robert ('Bowling Alone') Putnam, makes this point regarding Warren's Saddleback specifically: 'Orange County is virtually a desert in social-capital terms. The rate of mobility is really high. It has long and anonymous commutes. It's a very friendless place, and this church offers serious heavy friendship.'[51] Even churches of relatively moderate size normally provide crèches, media outlets, youth programmes, if not restaurants, gyms, sports teams and clubs for various activities. They offer opportunity and support. I once heard Joyce Meyer of Joyce Meyer Ministries boast revealingly to her enormous congregation: 'What I'm giving you this morning you couldn't get on the psychiatrist's couch for $10,000.' Wolfe notes the help such churches give so many women to adapt to the pressures of modern American living.[52] He notes the dieting programmes helping women make themselves attractive; he lists books like Don Colbert's *What Would Jesus Eat? The Ultimate Program for Eating Well, Feeling Great, and Living Longer*; Colleen Zuck and Elaine Meyer's *Daily Word for Weight Loss: Spiritual Guidance to Give You Courage on Your Journey*; and Jan Christiansen's *More of Him, Less of Me: My Personal Thoughts, Inspirations and Meditations on the Weight Down Diet*. Wolfe notes, writing in 2004, that this 'Weight Down Diet' 'had become such an integral part of congregational life in evangelical circles that by one estimate 10,000 churches feature it'.[53]

Consider just one other example of this thinking, the roadshow *Success 1994* which swept through major US cities, featuring famous athletes, famous preachers, military heroes (Norman Schwarzkopf, Colin Powell), the Governor of New York, and three former US Presidents (Ronald Reagan, George H. W. Bush, Gerald Ford), to enormous crowds paying up to $200 each for eight hours of 'all-American self-improvement'. A *Time* essay called this *Success 1994* roadshow 'part revival meeting, *The Music Man* and medicine-show and all uplift, with dialogue inspired by the Bible, *Poor Richard's Almanac*, Calvinism, common sense and Horatio Alger'. The organiser, son of Canadian missionaries, stated that 'the way to change a life is to stand up straight and say: "Lord Jesus, I need you. I want you to be number one in my life."' It all seemed 'harmless enough', really boiling down to making lists, setting goals and writing them down every day. The message was: 'You were born to win. But to be a winner, you must plan to win, expect to win.' The *Time* essayist concluded that *Success 1994* comprised 'essentially a secular religion preached by believing Christians'.[54] Once again, we should note the adjective 'believing' gratuitously attached to 'Christian', without any attempt to give it meaning.

Christian universities

The vast majority of American universities and colleges began life as denominational foundations. They vary enormously, not least in size, and there have been many more; at one stage Catholic colleges, especially colleges for women, were disappearing at the rate of one a week.[55] However, over time, they have almost all become secularised, or adopted the ethos of the surrounding milieu, even if at different speeds. Many severed links with their sponsoring churches early on: the Catholics' 'crazy season' came in the 1960s and 1970s,[56] some Missouri Synod colleges secularised in the 1970s, the Christian Reformed only at the turn of the millennium. The disaffiliation is well caught in the title of Burtchaell's survey of the phenomenon, *The Dying of the Light: The Disengagement of Colleges and Universities from Their Christian Churches*. Burtchaell's study covers many denominations—Congregational, Presbyterian, Methodist, Baptist, Lutheran, Catholic and Evangelical—and in ample and fascinating detail which allows for distinctiveness; among Evangelicals, for example, colleges of a Holiness origin have tended to stress morality (the morality of dancing is a recurrent theme) at the expense of doctrine, though neglecting doctrine is an accusation that could never be laid against the Christian Reformed. In all, however, the process has been inexorable.

Burtchaell's argument is that the colleges and universities secularised themselves—providing great scope for his irony. His study of the Presbyterian Davidson College stands for so many. In 1838 the faculty had to take the same 'vows' as Presbyterian clergy. By 1904 requirements were that a professor be a 'Christian gentleman' who never smoked, swore or imbibed. As Presbyterians became harder to find, Davidson became 'much more concerned that a man shall be a positive Christian and exercise Christian influence over young men' (1921). By 1945 one-fourth of the tenured professors might belong to any

Evangelical church. By 1957 all faculty except professors of Bible and philosophy were held only to a vague vow that (in Burtchaell's words) 'anyone but a Rosicrucian could accept'. By 1964 Davidson looked for 'genuine spirituality', 'humane instincts' and 'Christian character' in its faculty. By 1972 Davidson faculty had to appear 'prepared conscientiously to uphold and increase its effectiveness as an institution of Christian learning'. By 1974 one could be a 'reverent seeker' who would respect the Christian tradition without necessarily accepting it. By 1996 the president was the only person on the Davidson campus who had to belong to the Presbyterian Church.[57]

Since 'sectarianism' is seen as the great evil, and 'pluralism' and 'diversity' the desired aims, a Jesuit university president affirms: 'It would not be a good thing to have an all-Catholic board, an all-Catholic administration, faculty, staff and student body.'[58] Even that doesn't compete with New Rochelle whose aims became meaningless: 'values which motivated the founding ... openness to the shape of the future ... quest for meaning in life ... sensitivity to human dignity ... growth in self acceptance'.[59] This 'degraded rhetoric ... is more delusional than deceitful'. It bespeaks 'an ardent conviction that the college's educational purposes have remained the same, only now they are being pursued more sagaciously. Those who speak this way are being beguiled more than anyone who cares to listen.'[60]

Contributing to the disaffiliation was the need for funds, as colleges and universities sought more abundant funding outside their founding body (as the Baptist Wake Forest sought from the Reynolds tobacco family, and the Methodist Trinity (later Duke) from the Duke family), but above all from the public purse—the rhetoric so often changed according as it was directed at the founding denomination or at the state or funding bodies. As alumni were put on trustee boards (a move not unconnected to the funding issue) they too advanced the disaffiliation process. Presidents played a big part in their determination to imitate the academic pacesetters, all of them state and independent universities. Even colleges founded to train clergy had soon to recruit beyond their denominational base, and students wanted professional courses leading to careers rather than theology. Funding bodies pushed this trend further (for example, the Carnegie Foundation's refusal of grants to colleges requiring denominational quotas from any particular 'sect'). Above all, the disaffiliation process depended on the faculty, hired for their specialisms, with any attention to religious adherence inexorably receding; it was the faculty members' silence, indifference and eventually even hostility that finally swung it.[61]

What is interesting for my purposes here is that Burtchaell obviously regards this entire trajectory as unintended, unnecessary, and a disaster. The disengagement was based on mistakes and errors (a recurrent motif is that the process often occasioned misgiving, but usually only years—even decades—after decisions had been made which rendered the entire process irreversible). Burtchaell blames churches as much as the colleges; they were not determined enough and in many cases not equipped to preserve the denominational link (Catholic bishops could be as inept in this regard as anti-intellectual Baptist preachers with a distaste for learning because 'it must inevitably corrupt piety'). Burtchaell's alternative is clear enough: the churches should have been forming 'learned and articulate believers who were not only open to all truth, but possessed of advantages in approaching all truth: graced master insights, an interpretative community, and an authentic tradition'.[62] But this is the interesting part: to the extent that Burtchaell sees a cause of this failure, it is the entire trajectory of Christianity in the West over the last few hundred years—in terms of our argument here, the entire Western intellectual tradition over that time.[63]

Burtchaell can lament 'the failure of nerve, the deviance of purpose, and the degradation of public discourse', and 'the failures of the past, so clearly patterned, foolishly ignored and so lethally repeated',[64] but what other possibilities were there? What was the future for denominational colleges that didn't seek excellence in specialised appointments? Burtchaell himself plots the inexorable transition with an imaginary example. In 1870 Mr Jones might be a professor of mathematics in a Christian college, with duties anywhere in natural sciences. His son, Mr Jones, might be hired in 1900 as professor of chemistry. His son, Dr Jones, in 1930 might teach only organic chemistry. His son, Dr Jones, might in 1960 specialise in polymer chemistry. His daughter, Dr Jones, in the 1990s might be hired as a protein chemist; and she might shift institutions three or four times in her career to find her niche, unlike her great-great-grandfather who stayed at one college all his life.[65] How was such a move towards specialisation to be avoided?

Similarly with other developments like co-education or the commercialisation of sport. Of course, many colleges exist in the United States which attempt to resist this secularising trend and strive to renounce everything else in their quest for denominational purity, but their recruitment numbers tell their own story. Of the nearly 250 Catholic colleges in America, the fiercely traditionalist Cardinal Newman Society (established in 1993 'to promote and defend Catholic education') recommends in 2017 only 18. These 18 include Christendom College (student roll 477), John Paul the Great University (227), Northeast Catholic College (90), St Gregory's University (404), Thomas Aquinas College (389), the Thomas More College of Liberal Arts (92), and Wyoming Catholic College (155). The total number of students at the 18 (including the Catholic University of America, controlled by the Catholic Bishops of America and the largest with 3,241) is 19,741.[66] Georgetown alone has 18,000.

More fundamentally, Burtchaell laments that just as theology was getting into a position where it could address issues of American life, 'a great failure of nerve' set in and 'colleges and universities implicitly decided that serious theology was not appropriate' and they themselves marginalised theological discourse.[67] But this is too simple. The initiative was not only on the supply side; the demand was simply not there.[68]

Of course, there remains room for flagship Christian colleges like Wheaton, Notre Dame, Calvin (besides the reactive colleges like the Catholic ones mentioned immediately above), but surely American culture and society have triumphed. Burtchaell's lament is that the colleges could and should have stood back and critiqued the surrounding culture, rather than (as in fact happened) assimilating to the academy and American culture generally 'and [judging] gospel by the culture'.[69]

The same issue of secularisation of Christian colleges and universities is addressed in a slightly different way by (most prominently) Marsden, with his advocacy of 'Christian scholarship'. He begins *The Outrageous Idea of Christian Scholarship*: 'Contemporary University culture is hollow at its core.'[70] 'Today nonreligious viewpoints hold the advantage in academia so that something very much like "secular humanism" is informally established as much as Christianity was in the nineteenth century.'[71] His position is that Christians should be able to give their perspective; all others can—Marxists, feminists, gays, African

Americans—so why not Christians? Academic life, he argues, would be enriched by this additional perspective. Yet his argument is not perfectly clear. In the last analysis he seems to be saying that although a research-er's Christianity must not invalidate the methods and procedures accepted within individual academic disciplines, it could nevertheless have a bearing on motivation, perspective, agenda and implications (for example, a Christian scholar might save from oblivion a small religious group that mainline historical scholarship has ignored). Who could object to that? Yet much of the book obscures that central thrust (if such it is). He claims: 'Broadly understood, faith in something or other informs all scholarship. So the phrase "faith-informed" emphasizes that belief systems built around organized religious faiths should in principle have equal standing with other worldviews.'[72] But that is tendentious. Just because every academic has not personally established the first prin-ciples from which his discipline operates, that hardly legitimates a spe-cifically 'Christian' revision of the accepted procedures of any disci-pline.[73] What indeed would Christian history or archaeology or linguistics or physics look like? How would they proceed? And in fact, 'Christian' is not a simple term; does Marsden mean in effect 'Evangelical'? Marsden seems well aware of all the difficulties associated with his 'Christian scholarship'. He concedes everything, but then car-ries on as though the concessions mean nothing.[74]

The problems underlying 'Christian scholarship' are well illustrated by those colleges militantly fighting back. The 115 members (pre-dominantly Reformed in character) of the Council of Christian Colleges and Universities have established a 'Conference of Faith and History' to preserve a particularly 'Christian' historiography. Their concept of 'Christian history' contains some strands which would be perfectly acceptable in today's wider academy (for example, as I think Marsden seems to advocate, allowing proper scope for the religious motivation of historical actors rather than reducing everything to eco-nomic or political factors, or letting faith influence one's choice of topic), but other strands are far more problematic. One such prob-lematic strand is to use history to find Christian moral values verified over ages. Another is to show that history confirms Christianity's historical claims. A third is to trace God's providence in history. Surely these 'Christian' strands merely bring history as a recognised academic discipline to a juddering halt.[75] It is hard to see how such tendentious inquiry could find any place in American universities as they have come to exist.

Burtchaell's study does not cover John Paul II's 1990 *Ex corde ecclesiae*, a demand from Rome to reverse the secularisation of Catholic universities. Initially American's Catholic bishops had voted (by 224 votes to 6) to implement the Vatican directive by 'consultation and dialogue' with America's nearly 250 Catholic institutions of higher education. The Vatican rejected this, and, specifically targeting *America's* higher education sector, insisted that the bishops adopt the papal norms in full,[76] which the American bishops in 1999 dutifully did, reversing by 223 to 31 votes their policy of three years earlier. *Ex corde ecclesiae* has raised the issue of identity in a new way, but this document was not the only factor in bringing a university's religious identity to the fore. Steinfels for one had already made this issue his own, interviewing educationalists across the continent, teaching at both Georgetown and Notre Dame between 1994 and 2001, and at both serving on special committees to enhance Catholic identity. He outlines measures to reverse the trend. For Steinfels (as for many others), the problem is that the benchmark secular colleges and universities are taken as the only model of academic excellence. Catholic universities should set out to be different, and hire according to four norms: being clear about their mission; distinguishing between hiring for Catholic identity and hiring Catholics; embedding concerns about the religious dimension into the whole hiring process and beyond; and avoiding mechanical or inflexible rules. What counts 'is the *overall pattern of vibrant engagement* with Catholic concerns and traditions in the intellectual and communal life of the institution'.[77]

Much of his reflection is immensely sophisticated (even if some of the more aspirational rhetoric would expose him to Burtchaell's irony), but Steinfels underestimates the challenge posed by the new consciousness associated with modernity. He supposes that this Catholic character is something all can recognise and pursue. While Thomism lasted, Catholic universities embodied something distinctive because they had to hand a philosophy that encompassed all. But Thomism collapsed around the 1960s. Today, the issue is well caught in Gleason's comment on Catholic universities: 'The crisis is not that Catholic educators do not want their institutions to remain Catholic, but that they are no longer sure what remaining Catholic means.'[78] The problem of identity goes far beyond institutions; more fundamentally, it affects the people making up these established institutions. Steinfels himself quotes 'any number of undergraduates at Notre Dame and Georgetown' in the 1990s: 'I like being a Catholic. I'm proud to be a Catholic. But I don't really know what being a Catholic means.'[79] And Christian Smith, himself at Notre Dame, seems to agree, demonstrating that the Catholics at this flagship institution are little different from their non-Catholic peers in their vague 'religiosity'. He reached the conclusion that even of those touting their 'religiosity', relatively few 'engaged in any meaningful way with the Catholic religious tradition'.[80]

The problem, as I have been concerned to show throughout, is the instinctive understanding of 'the real' in the modern West. Burtchaell would have probably seen *Ex corde ecclesiae* and much of the ensuing debate as one more lament decades too late, but it is surely much more; it is an appeal to a cognitive style that no longer has much purchase.[81] With the cognitive shift of the last few centuries, knowledge has been largely understood to be built on observation, evidence and experiment, with no circumscribed data and no idea or value any longer allowed to claim acceptance by virtue of its origins. Intellectual inquiry now excludes claims to cognitive privilege on the part of accepted traditions or established practices, even more so of divine revelation. This cognitive style must infuse any serious research institution, as distinct from one merely socialising youth into an existing community. That is the plight of America's denominational universities.

Obama's religion

One issue that perfectly focuses the issues underlying claims of 'American exceptionalism' is the debate on the religion of President Obama.[82] Obama's portrait of his mother's religion is illustrative of the issues under discussion here. Although avowedly secularist, his mother was the most 'spiritually awakened' person he ever met. She was invariably kind and loving, and acted on those instincts even when it was not in her own interests. Independently of scriptures or religious authorities, she instilled in her son values like discipline, honesty, hard work, and sensitivity to the feelings of others—values that other Americans might well learn in Sunday school. All her life she inveighed against poverty and injustice, and was fiercely critical of those who simply accepted them.

'Most of all, she possessed an abiding sense of wonder, a reverence for life and its precious transitory nature that could properly be described as devotional. During the course of the day, she might come across a painting, read a line of poetry, or hear a piece of music, and I would see tears well up in her eyes. Sometimes, as I was growing up, she would wake me up in the middle of the night to have me gaze at a particularly spectacular moon, or she would have me close my eyes as we walked together at twilight to listen to the rustle of leaves ... She saw mysteries everywhere and took joy in the sheer strangeness of life.

'It is only in retrospect, of course, that I fully understand how deeply this spirit of hers influenced me ... It was my mother's fundamental faith—in the goodness of people and in the ultimate value of this brief life we've each been given, that channeled [my] ambitions ... and it was in search of some practical application of those values that I accepted work after college as a community organizer for a group of churches in Chicago that were trying to cope with joblessness, drugs and hopelessness in their midst.'[83]

That's all well and good, even admirable and inspiring, but it does illustrate the complexity of discussing religion in America. Wonder, mystery and awe, concern for others, discipline, industry and so on often flow from religious beliefs, not least Christian beliefs, but such a source is not necessary; there is no reason why any of these need indicate something substantively religious. Obama in this passage admits that it was religion *in his mother's sense* that led him to work for a group of black churches.[84] I have not seen evidence to show that his religious views changed. Christopher Hitchens, reviewing a biography of Obama, notes: '[The author] doesn't say enough about a question that fascinates me and enrages the American right: the possibility that the president of the United Sates is not a Muslim, but, worse, an unbeliever.'[85] The fact that Obama made 'Christian' utterances in public appearances proves little; no American President can afford not to (as became evident in the candidacy of Donald Trump).[86] Simon Perfect gives a particularly generous summation of Obama's religion: 'His public rhetoric became more explicitly Christian and more theologically orthodox during his presidency. This reflected both his apparently deepening private faith and his manipulation of its public expression as a political tool.'[87] This may well be the case, but Perfect provides little evidence for the deepening private faith, and in a quest for 'parsimony of explanation', it is not unreasonable to concentrate on the political manipulation.

Conclusion

The 2005 National Study of Youth and Religion (NSYR) reveals, even among American youth asserting their church affiliation and attendance, a transformation from the substantive teaching of traditional Christianity towards what is called 'Moralistic Therapeutic Deism' (MTD), which Davie has called a benign, relatively undemanding and noticeably content-lite form of Christianity.[88] There is no need to go on. The Older Berger implicitly (and rather confusingly, since he had by then repudiated the secularisation thesis) seemed to agree that so much of American Christianity has been hollowed out or internally secularised. Writing in 2011, he acknowledged that what was common to the themes repudiated by the earlier 1975 *Hartford Appeal for Theological Affirmation* (for which he was largely responsible) 'was that they proposed an understanding of Christianity divested of its transcendent (or, if you will, cosmic or supernatural) core. Conversely, they reinterpreted Christianity as a moral code, a therapeutic instrument, or a political agenda. All these themes were accommodations to a secularism dominant in elite culture.'[89] Observers like the former editor of *The Economist* who glibly talk about the 'return of God', claiming that 'the great forces of modernity ... are all strengthening religion rather than undermining it', might well pay more attention to what so many of these churches actually stand for.[90]

5

THE FUTURE

Just what changes are possible within a religious tradition? How malleable are they? How much can a 'memory mutate' while maintaining the character of the original? In preserving the 'historical continuity of systems of symbols',[1] how far can the continuity be stretched? The notion of identity persisting through change is not simple. The problem can be glimpsed here: 'This is my grandfather's axe; my father replaced the handle and I replaced the blade.' The point is captured in a more sophisticated form in Neurath's image of being at sea on a ship of which we can repair any part that seems to need it but never the whole of the ship at the same time, since we have to retain some foothold on it.[2] However, although change can obviously be profound, the notion of change can perhaps be pushed too far. In at least some cases, the very concept of change may be unhelpful. It may be more analytically fruitful to invoke complete disjunction, or to admit that we have dispensed with what we had and replaced it with something entirely different— or, indeed, have dispensed with what we had and have not replaced it with anything.

There is a contemporary debate about possible limits of change within religious traditions. Halliday is one who has argued that all major religions are a reservoir of values, symbols and ideas from which it is possible to derive virtually anything: 'As one Iranian thinker put it, Islam is a sea in which it is possible to catch almost any fish one wants.'

Bruce, by contrast, argues that just because there can be considerable variation between the public expressions of a particular religion, it does not follow that infinite variation is possible. To pursue Halliday's image, different seas nurture different fish, depending on whether the waters are fresh or salt, warm or cool, deep or shallow.[3]

A recent restatement of the 'limited possibilities' position is that of Peel, who attempts to allow for the diverse ways in which people recognise themselves as belonging to a religious tradition, while insisting that the tradition does not permit development in any direction whatsoever. For Peel, in a religion's constant interplay with contemporary issues, the tradition provides a heavy 'steer'. Peel's conclusion is essentially Cook's: 'No religious heritage is a reliable predictor of the behavior of those who inherit it, but just as surely heritages are not interchangeable.'[4]

However, these authors are all writing of changes in pre-modern circumstances, like those presumed in Küng's paradigms mentioned at the beginning of chapter 2. Even in those pre-modern cases, I would argue that religious change is not an issue that can be resolved theoretically or a priori. It can be resolved only by attending to what happened in fact. We remarked in chapter 1 that scriptures, often taken to be the charter determining possible future expressions of a religion, can be reduced to a blank page on which one can write what one needs to. It is surely the same for traditions. Tony Judt has pithily claimed: 'A Protestant who does not believe in the Scriptures, a Catholic who abjures the authority of the Pope in Rome ... these are incoherent categories.'[5] Yes, provided one realises that the Bible for Protestants and the papacy for Catholics have been, when required, effectively remade to order.

The change we have been addressing in this book is, however, of another order altogether. (There is, of course, the quite different question whether something is a legitimate change or perversion, but that has not been our concern here.) For us, the question has rather been whether something is best conceptualised as a change in what was there before, or its complete evacuation or evisceration. For my purposes, and I have tried to be consistent throughout, religion involves some relation to superhuman powers—which the authors just quoted have not required (even Bruce, normally so insistent on a substantive understanding). My argument has been that Christianity in the West, understood substantively, has been effectively evacuated. It is only by slipping from a substantive to a functional understanding that this reality can be obscured.

It is hard to avoid the conclusion that traditional Christianity is running on borrowed time, or (to change the metaphor) constitutes a case of 'wasting capital'. Alasdair MacIntyre raised the spectre of language (in his case, that of morality) which amounts to little more than a collection of verbal remains. 'What we possess ... are the fragments of a conceptual scheme, parts which now lack those contexts from which their significance derived ... we continue to use many of the key expressions. But we have—very largely, if not entirely—lost our comprehension, both theoretical and practical, of [the reality they originally expressed].' Collini paraphrases MacIntyre: we are deploying 'an inherited vocabulary without the underlying assumptions that for a long time made sense of it'.[6]

Fukuyama, describing our world today, can speak of its dependence on 'the ghosts of dead religious beliefs, if not those beliefs themselves'.[7] A readiness to speak of 'dead religious beliefs' can perhaps be more fruitful than speaking of developed or mutated religious beliefs.

The great ditch

It seems safe to say that the shift traced here, the rise of a new cognitive style, constitutes a watershed; many would say *the* watershed in the history of humankind.[8] This shift has changed the conditions of human life. Up till about 1800, the standard of living on all continents was roughly the same; very low indeed by today's measure. Before then, economic growth based on technological change barely existed. But the intellectual environment that gave rise to natural science, the application of science and technology to production and its accompanying refinements, have produced continuous innovation and increase.[9] This shift has been so powerful that it has swept all before it—so much so that it could enable Britain (in Seeley's expression) to acquire an empire 'in a fit of absence of mind'.

The idea of a 'great ditch' seems far more convincing than an approach like Fried's, according to which everything we have now is clearly built on what was already there in the Middle Ages. Yes, demarcation of periods can be forced, and one thing does lead on to another, and it is helpful to point out the glimmerings of things that later came to fruition; but granting all that, it is still possible that someone today looking at the differences between, say, the 1300s and the 2000s would be struck not by the similarities but by the dissimilarities. Yes, Marco Polo did (perhaps) get to China, and if you want to call that the beginnings of globalisation, fine; but in our world of multinationals, transnational political bodies, mass migrations, unregulated and instantaneous flow of capital, surely globalisation means something rather different. Fried's comments on social contracts in Carolingian times capture his approach: 'The deep-seated roots of Western notions of constitutional rule, power sharing, codetermination, and democracy that would come to shape European history in the modern period all derive ultimately from this tradition.'[10] Ultimately perhaps; but what strikes most observers is the great ditch of the seventeenth century and later.

The claim to a watershed is not made in arrogance. There is ample room for both apprehension and humility. The reasons for the shift may be in large measure fortuitous, even if momentous in consequences. Mokyr, in comparing the scientific revolution in Europe with the situation in China in the same period, puts it well: 'It seems wrong to dub the Chinese experience a "failure". What is exceptional, indeed unique, is what happened in eighteenth-century Europe.'[11]

It is undeniable that in recent centuries in Europe the radically different worldview formulated by the sciences, spearheaded by astronomy, became disconnected from a religious understanding of reality. The religious was 'shifting from the realm of information to a realm more like that of mythology. In this way the old mind could live on alongside the new, in a less central way and in a different key.'[12]

This 'different key' idea has given rise to the notion of NOMA or 'non-overlapping magisteriums'.[13] In this view, science and religion operate on totally different planes, which by definition never intersect. Scientific propositions deal with the world out there; religious statements are something else, addressing ultimate questions and expressing moral values. Richard Dawkins objects violently to what he considers this subterfuge; religion, along with its values and morality, always attempted to explain reality (what I have called the inevitable cognitive element of religion), and this explaining was done in terms of otherworldly forces.[14] My argument has been that such explanations, though not discredited, have been marginalised by a far more powerful form of explanation; a new mind has displaced the old mind.

'Those who still fully *lived* the old mind, however, whatever their numbers, were now in the margins of things: the new mind was developing the technologies and social structure that were transforming the world.'[15] It is this new worldview 'that drives almost everything of significance that happens in our world, from technologies to economies, with the resulting impact on the social and political organization of *almost* all societies, even the ones where the majority of people still hold to a version of the pre-seventeenth-century mind-set'.[16]

Multiple modernities

This persistence of the marginalised worldview in the modern world raises its own issues. 'Modern' certainly means more than just existing in the twenty-first century. Modernisation means something like

> that combination of changes—in the mode of production and government, in the social and institutional order, in the corpus of knowledge, and in attitudes and values—that makes it possible for a society to hold its own in the twenty-first century; that is, to compete on even terms in the generation of material and cultural wealth, to sustain its independence, and to promote and accommodate to further change.[17]

Modernity is obviously not a simple notion; components of modernity seem to include power-driven machinery, integrated transport systems, science, technology and research and development, financial services, standardisation of weights, measures and currencies, systems of public health, attention to the status of women, universal education, leisure, consumerism, state-run welfare, political parties, trades unions, civil service and bureaucracy, social legislation, organised sport, conscript military forces, and (increasingly, in all its ramifications) electronic communication. Of course, many elements are far from positive: other characteristics are organised crime, inequality, an underclass, and weaponry with destructive power beyond the comprehension of previous ages.[18] Above all, though, our cognitive shift must be part of it—indeed, most of these things are made possible only through this shift.

There is a lively debate about whether there is one modernity or multiple modernities. Much of the discussion concerns religion: to what extent can one be modern and understand reality religiously? Berger has written: 'Modernization is not a unilinear process leading to a Western-type society ... There is no single type of modernity ... There are wide variations possible within these structures—indeed, a kaleidoscope of cultural possibilities.'[19] But Berger is confused. He invariably insists on a substantive understanding of religion, but has slipped here to another level altogether, or into a cultural mode. Japan, Berger continues, was 'the first non-Western country to modernize successfully, while maintaining many elements of its traditional culture'.[20] Yes, the Japanese eat with chopsticks, watch sumo on TV, and increasingly wear kimonos for high school graduation, but that is not in conflict with the argument of this book, which has attempted to differentiate culture from religion. Berger seems to suggest that, if while at your computer you wear a Mandela shirt, have salsa music playing in the background, and take time off to eat curry or sushi, you have demonstrated multiple modernities.[21] Such cultural elements are beside the point. The point is that one cannot be modern and think that malaria is caused by witchcraft or that AIDS can be cured with incantations.

To make this point is not to imply some moral superiority of the modern. Nor is it some glorification of a particular sector of humanity over others. Nor is it to make some 'racist, they've-just-come-down-from-the-trees kind of argument'.[22] The 'shocking inequality of power of diverse cognitive styles' is the defining fact of our times.[23]

> You cannot understand the human condition if you ignore or deny its total transformation by the success of the scientific revolution ... [This] has totally transformed the terms of reference in which human societies operate. To pretend that the scientific revolution of the seventeenth century, and its eventual application in the later stage of the industrial revolution have not transformed the world but are merely changes from one culture to another, is simply an irresponsible affectation.[24]

The significant thing about this new mindset is that it is *not* restricted to particular peoples, but is transcultural; this 'cognitive strategy [would be] the correct strategy in *any* world'.[25] It is not 'Western' in any hard sense, like 'in Western genes', for as we have seen it has come to the West only recently, haltingly and fortuitously. Other forms of knowing cannot compete:

> One particular style of knowledge has proved so overwhelmingly powerful, economically, militarily, administratively, that all societies have had to make their peace with it and adopt it. Some have done it more successfully than others, and some more willingly or more quickly than others; but all of them have had to do it, or perish. Some have retained more, and some less, of their previous cultures.[26]

Recognition of this cognitive shift is unavoidable if we are to understand the world today. I briefly sketched the 'enchanted religious imagination' or 'cosmic religion' in chapter 2. Awareness of different cognitive styles has considerable bearing on one's understanding of the enormous development industry. Development as commonly understood, in education, health, transport, agriculture and finance, is the attempt to foster a shift from a religious understanding of reality—an understanding in terms of spiritual forces—to a rationality of functional instrumentality.[27] (That is a better way of putting it than describing the shift as one from irrationality to rationality, because the enchanted religious imagination can have its own form of highly elaborate rationality within the parameters of its own assumptions.) But development does involve cognitive engineering at a fairly profound level, bringing about a shift from one way of experiencing reality to another. Education today encompasses physics, chemistry, biology or statistics with the aim of providing another repertoire of causality. In health, causality is sought in microbes or bacteria rather than witchcraft. Transport requires roads built on the basis of surveying and engineering; air travel is concerned with technology, maintenance, budgeting and marketing—rather than, say, exorcism of evil spirits to which the management of Ghana Airways resorted to prevent the airline's impending collapse.[28] Agriculture is concerned with fertilisers, crop rotation and irrigation, and avoids attributing poor seasons to ancestral curses, or abundance to fertility rituals. Wealth is created through things like effort, budgeting, double-entry bookkeeping, innovation and manufacturing rather than obtained by animal or even human sacrifice. Of course health, education, transport, agriculture and finance are not exact sciences, and anyone can cite numerous cases of ignorance, mistakes and (most likely) unintended consequences. The best contemporary development is enormously alert to cultural sensitivities. But the point remains that development in all these areas involves a shift from one worldview to another, from a religious to a secular understanding of reality.

This does not commit me to the discredited modernisation theory (though, as I have suggested in the case of secularisation, theories are sometimes not as discredited as accepted wisdom would have it). Modernisation theory, stemming from thinkers like Marx, Durkheim, Tönnies and Weber, tended to argue that modernisation was not only a good thing, but all of a piece. The good things of modernisation came together: economic development, different social relationships (away from kinship groups), education, the shift towards values like 'achievement' and rationality, and strong political institutions. Huntington's *Political Order in Changing Societies* showed that the components of modernity do not all go together; they need to be separated. The political, economic and social dimensions of development 'relate to one another as separate phenomena that periodically interact'.[29] Thus their inter-reaction elsewhere need not replicate the path Europe pioneered. The end result, however, must be much the same.

Current Christian landscape

The effect of this cognitive shift on the mainline Christian denominations has been profound. They were established on a mindset which has largely been eclipsed. Yet these denominations are not going away. Many remain institutionally important players. *The Economist* in 2012 estimated that the Cardinal Archbishop of New York is the biggest landowner in Manhattan, if one includes all the organisations that come under his jurisdiction. In the US, the Catholic Church has over 6,800 schools (5 per cent of the national total), 630 hospitals (11 per cent), a similar number of lesser health facilities, 244 colleges and universities. Many of these are distinguished for excellence: 7 of the leading 25 part-time law schools in America are Catholic, and a quarter of the 100 top-ranked hospitals are Catholic. Further, *The Economist* estimated (the Catholic Church itself does not disclose its finances) that spending by Catholic bodies was about $170 billion in 2010. Catholic institutions employ about one million people. For comparison, in 2010 General

Electric revenue was about $150 billion, and Walmart employed roughly two million people. The Catholic Church is America's largest single charitable organisation. Its main charity and its subsidiaries employ over 65,000 paid staff and serve over ten million people. In 2010 they distributed $4.7 billion to the poor.[30] Other denominations have their own significant institutions, although not proportionally—it was specifically anti-Catholicism that led the Catholic Church to create this parallel society in the nineteenth and twentieth centuries.

It is the same in other countries. The *New Yorker* claims that Catholic institutions own a quarter of all real estate in Rome, and 20 per cent of all real estate throughout Italy.[31] The Church of England's £7.9 billion investment fund, managed by the Church Commissioners for England with an in-house team of 35 investment professionals, made 17 per cent returns on investments in 2016, distinguishing itself as one of the world's strongest-performing endowment funds.[32] Spencer notes that 'There are nearly 50,000 faith-based charities in the UK, out of a total of nearly 188,000 registered charities. These charities receive 23%, or £16 billion, of the charity sector's income in England and Wales.'[33] And of course, Christian development arms are some of the biggest in the world (the Catholic Caritas, the Evangelical World Vision, the Lutheran World Federation); indeed, sponsoring their development activity is often a central activity of churches in the West. These Christian institutions make the churches public players of enormous importance, with interests and concerns that demand attention. Yet it must be admitted that they now function essentially as NGOs, pressure groups, institutions of civil society. This function is not to be underestimated, but one should note that it is not that traditionally claimed, which was relating the human to the otherworldly. Grace Davie has remarked: 'Mentalities endure, even when the institution has altered considerably.'[34] My point here is rather the opposite: the institution runs on, purportedly the same, although the rationale underlying it has been profoundly changed.[35]

The cultural clout of the historic Christian denominations remains immense, too, another area in which they are not going away anytime soon, even if again it represents an area of decreasing capital. Western literature, art and music are incomprehensible without them. One cannot visit a museum, art gallery, concert house or cathedral in Europe without being confronted with the Christian past. Endowed chairs of theology and philosophy in colleges and universities have helped preserve traditional thinking—perhaps rather more than current demand might require. (As we have also seen, though, the struggle of these Christian universities to preserve their 'identity' in the face of ambient American culture captures the predicament of Western religion today.)

Very often public bodies of inquiry will include a Christian minister of some sort. This seems widely accepted though New Atheists like Richard Dawkins can object vociferously. Even though their days are almost inevitably numbered, the presence of 26 Anglican bishops in Britain's House of Lords has not given rise to any significant campaign to remove them; it is widely accepted that many of them are capable, concerned, impartial and committed, with much to contribute (to contribute, of course, in line with the argument of this book, on the basis of secular expertise and not episcopal anointing).

Yet if we take the historically important issues of mainline Christianity; of Calvinism, say: unconditional election, limited atonement, total depravity, irresistible grace, perseverance of the saints; or of Lutheranism: justification, grace, faith, the Cross, the Bible and the two kingdoms; or of Catholicism: sacramentality, mediation, the communion of saints, tradition, we see immediately that they are no longer of much public moment. These issues are not dead, and at seminaries training the denomination's ministers, they will be thoroughly rehearsed. Their impact, however, beyond the seminary seems limited. In the public sphere, church authorities of all the liberal churches are reduced to addressing the same issues and in roughly the same terms, because all mainline Western denominations now operate within the parameters set by the surrounding culture, not Christian revelation or even denominational history (evident in our Lutheran theologian deploring his bishop's assimilation to the leaders of other denominations, mentioned at the end of chapter 3).

The churches as NGOs seems to satisfy many. John Allen's *The Future Church* purports to offer, as the title suggests, a picture of what global Catholicism is becoming.[36] He presents Catholicism, not as a tradition and an institution for conceptualising and relating to supernatural realities, but as a pressure group or lobby with a vision for improving this world. His book outlines possible Catholic contributions to living in harmony with Muslims, coping with ageing populations, living more equitably. There are chapters on biotechnology, globalisation and ecology, with detailed expositions on water wars, protecting the Amazon, preserving the traditions and cultures of indigenous peoples, a pro-Dalit crusade. In short, Catholicism is concerned with almost everything that Oxfam and UNICEF are. There is virtually nothing about how in the twenty-first century Catholics might conceptualise a supra-mundane realm, how they might relate to it, what living in such a relationship might require. His suggested Catholic involvement is religious only in the sense of 'performed by an institution historically religious'. Revealingly, it is in a comparison with Pentecostalism that he casually notes that different streams in Catholicism will have different 'attitudes towards the supernatural'.[37] That is one of the few hints in the book that Catholicism is anything more than a more cohesive United Nations. The NGO-isation of Christianity is complete.[38]

Newman could easily write of Catholics believing something that Protestants have trouble with.[39] In discussing miracles, he can talk as if there is a special Catholic understanding.[40] That seems impossible in the West now. Modern Western Catholics and Protestants have become assimilated. Even Kenny does not quite catch the completeness of this change. He writes: 'The differences between contemporary Catholics and Protestants on topics such as grace, justification, and free will are likely to be much less than those that separate both of them from the official positions laid out on either side of the Reformation controversies.'[41] He is making the seemingly undeniable point that today's attitudes to the issues of the Reformation are fairly undifferentiated, but he still talks of Catholics and Protestants in the West as identifiable and separate blocs with distinctive mindsets. Conversion has traditionally been a key Christian notion; the conversion evident today, even of those professing Christianity, is to modern Western culture.

Of course there are still forces resisting the shift (google any of America's traditional Catholic websites). Pope John Paul II insisted that proscribing women's ordination is not a question of misogyny or power but of fidelity to God's will; thus 'The Church has no authority whatsoever to confer priestly ordination on women and … this judgment is to be definitively held by all the Church's faithful'.[42] Pronouncing God's will and demanding adherence by fiat is anachronistic in an age of affluence, mass education and individualism (and indeed most indications are that in the West a majority of those identifying themselves as Catholics don't hold his view). Similarly, Cardinal Pell's explanation of why the Catholic Church will not change its position on homosexuality or divorce—'This kind of shift is not ultimately possible within the Catholic Church'[43]—is no longer the cognitive style of modernity, where evidence and experience trump tradition every time. The attempt to resist is perhaps behind the drive to elevate Newman, beatified by Pope Benedict XVI in 2010. For Newman, the tradition of the church was definitive: 'Ecclesiastical authority, not argument is the supreme rule and the appropriate guide for Catholics in matters of religion ... it is an ipso facto confutation of any reasonings inconsistent with it.'[44] And: 'If we would solve new questions, it must be by consulting old answers.'[45] He deplored 'the undervaluing of Antiquity, and resting on one's own reasonings, judgments, definitions etc, rather than authority and precedent'.[46] Such an attitude to the past is virtually impossible today.

Marginalisation in the West

Bruce has drawn attention to 'professional interest' as a gauge of the significance of religion. He argues that compared with 1800, 1850, 1900 or even 1950, the attention paid to religion is now minuscule. A study of the middle classes between 1780 and 1850 begins with three chapters on religion. By comparison, a standard British text on contemporary society has chapters on cities, education, work, women and the division of labour, elites and privilege, deviance and the law, and social welfare, but no chapter on religion. 'Experts on these topics manage to write at length without mentioning religion at all.'[47] Of course, this is less so of the US, but, as suggested above, the treatment of 'religion' there might often be more constructively pursued in terms of politics or culture than in terms of religion in our sense.

The decline is perhaps even more evident in biography and autobiography. Consider Noel Annan's *Our Age*, ideal for our purposes because it deals with those who controlled Britain between 1945 and 1990, and seeks to answer the question: since this was the period of Britain's decline, were they responsible? Annan argues that those constituting the 'establishment' were cultured and intellectual but were far less proficient at practical application of the solutions they devised, and valued consensus above all. What is of interest for us is the role of religion. Annan insists that at his public school, Stowe, 'One subject was ... taught thoroughly. That was Christianity.'[48] Yet for all the issues Annan raises, Christianity seems simply irrelevant. His chapter on 'How Our Age Discussed Morality' (dealing prominently with changing attitudes to homosexuality) actually begins by noting: 'Religion no longer gave us a large-scale explanation of life.'[49]

It is not my intention to pile up examples, because selecting them is necessarily subjective, but this verdict seems fairly pervasive. Kenneth Clark ('Lord Clark of Civilization'), steeped in Christianity, surprising even himself that 'my history of civilization has really turned into a history of religion',[50] saw Christianity as our glorious past, not something to be embraced now. John Carey, Merton Professor of English Literature at Oxford, was equally steeped in Christianity, but as our illustrious heritage, not a serious option for today:

> Studying seventeenth-century English literature was really the same as studying Christianity. That was all they seriously cared about, and they cared enough, at a pinch, to kill or be killed for their own particular brand of it. I was excited by this. As a lapsed Christian I felt I could imagine—just—how it would be to believe as they believed. At heart I knew this was a delusion.[51]

The persons just mentioned may be considered elite, but Callum Brown, co-director of the Scottish Oral History Centre at the University of Strathclyde, corroborates the marginalisation of Christianity in the lives of ordinary people. One of his most significant contributions is using the notion of discursivity from cultural studies—the study of narrative structures to reveal how societies imagine themselves—to argue that from 1800 to 1960 people drew heavily on Christian tracts, Christian morality and Christian narrative structure to tell their own life stories. It was a Christian narrative which individuals used to reveal their identity. A comparison of the narratives of generations born successively around 1900, 1930 and 1960 shows how this Christian discourse came to disappear. Christian identity broke down around the 1960s when new media, new gender roles and moral revolution dramatically ended people's conception that they lived Christian lives; it was not only associational or institutional links they came to lose, but (more significantly for Brown) discursive links with Christianity.[52]

Berger gives considerable importance in understanding our Western world today to the categories he labels 'Davos culture' and 'faculty club culture'. Davos culture refers to the international culture of business and political leaders, and not just to those who are actually invited to gatherings at Davos, but the millions who would like to receive an invitation, those characterised by the economic and political values of the yuppie *internationale*. 'Faculty club culture' refers to the Western intelligentsia found in academic networks, foundations, media, NGOs, and embodying ideologies like human rights, environmentalism, feminism, multiculturalism and third-worldism. These movements can be referenced in shorthand by their headquarters, respectively the Washington of the World Bank and IMF, and New York's East 43rd St, the seat of the Ford Foundation.[53] But probably even more suggestive of current dynamics is a possible third category that we can term 'smartphone culture', with its own values, values like technological one-upmanship, entertainment, communication, immediacy, innovation, obsolescence and (some might add) superficiality. Not only is this third culture more diffuse, even if centred in the US like the other two (its headquarters Cupertino?), but it is also even more dissociated from religion. One can hear voices stressing the indispensable Christian underpinning of the 'Davos culture' (Weigel's 'Capitalism is the only Catholic system'), as also of 'faculty club culture' (the encyclical *Laudato si'*), but it would be hard to find similar claims for the 'smartphone culture'.

The future of religion

My argument here has not been that of Dawkins or Hitchens that 'religion poisons everything', to cite the subtitle of Hitchens's attack. Not many would share the sentiment sometimes attributed to Gibbon on passing Chartres cathedral: 'I paused only to dart a look of contempt at the stately pile of superstition and passed on.' It is hard to disagree with J.M. Roberts in *Triumph of the West*: 'We could none of us today be what we are if a handful of Jews nearly two thousand years ago had not believed that they had known a great teacher, seen him crucified, dead, and buried, and then rise again.'[54] And reflection stemming from this conviction has constituted a towering achievement: 'The creation of this [medieval] synthesis, in which the developed beliefs and doctrines of Catholicism were boldly and brilliantly interpreted in terms of Greek thought, must rank as one of the greatest human feats of intellectual and imaginative construction ever achieved.'[55] For this reason, the rejection of any specific mention of Christianity in the 1994 draft European Union Constitution seems rather churlish. It is not that religion poisons everything, but that the experience of the last few hundred years has changed our situation utterly. A new mindset has arisen. The world operates on another plane from the understanding of pervasive otherworldly powers on which our civilisation was built.

What sometimes masks the changed status of Christianity in the West is that the principal denominations are almost all international bodies. Outside the West their membership is growing, and in large measure their new members are not so affected by Western history of recent centuries. This brings tensions, and now that immigration is such a feature of contemporary life, the picture can be even more confused. Migration can mask so much. An influx of Hispanics, Filipinos or Nigerians can skew statistics. Although their members may be in or from the global South, the cognitive centres of gravity of all the historic denominations remain firmly in the North. Jenkins has claimed that for demographic reasons, the official Catholic Church must espouse a 'Southern viewpoint', but this is simply not so.[56] As Comoro and Sivalon argue, against those claiming that the Second Vatican Council was opening up to all cultures, the council was in fact bringing Catholicism into line with the modern, Western world:

> The worldview and cosmology of pre-Vatican II Roman Catholicism were in fact an inculturated understanding based on a culture and consciousness very similar to traditional African culture. Vatican II, while marking an opening up to the world, was in fact opening up to a world, worldview and culture of modernity that are quite different from African culture. As the church accommodated itself to scientific and secularised culture it moved dramatically away from the cultures of indigenous people around the world.[57]

Some argue that religion must persist, because 'the need for religion appears to be hard-wired in the human animal'.[58] Bellah claims that

'Religion is a part of the species life of man, as central to his self-defi-
nition as speech'.[59] Britain's Chief Rabbi has claimed: '*Homo sapiens* is
the meaning seeking animal. Alone among life forms we ask the big
questions. Who am I? Why am I here? How then shall I live?' He argues
that four alternative sources of meaning have made an appearance in
recent centuries: the market, the state, science, philosophy. These four
have failed, and this 'has created the space which religion has returned
to fill, and which indeed it always did fill'.[60] Undoubtedly many are
seeking answers, but it seems undeniable that in the modern West a
good many seek what are to them satisfactory answers that are in no
way religious. Many seek fulfilment in creating a home and being a
good parent, excelling in one's profession, working to improve society
in some specific area. Fulfilment may come from pursuing goals on
what might be considered a slightly lower plane: promoting a favourite
daughter's ballet career, getting Russian up to a level where one can
read Solzhenitsyn in the original, restoring a crumbling farmhouse in
Burgundy. Some goals may be deemed decidedly lower, like making
ever more money, continually reducing one's golf handicap, or inces-
sant travel. It seems incontrovertible that meaning in life, to an extent
that makes life liveable, may not only not be religious in a traditional
sense, but not religious in any sense. (And this may be effectively the
case, even though in polls many may be tempted for reasons of self-
presentation to elevate the level on which they find meaning.)

As to our principal concern, although theoretically a reversal is possible, it seems certain that the hitherto accepted awareness of supernatural powers has been permanently eclipsed. Some dispute this. Thus
Fernández-Armesto, proclaiming a rosy future for religion, gives as the
first of five reasons: 'The unintelligible cosmos disclosed by postmodern science and philosophy will drive people back to the comforting
certainties of suprarational faiths.'[61] That seems merely perverse. So
does his second: 'In a morally deprived world, societies will need moral
dogma to survive and individuals will want peremptory guidance to
relieve their bewilderment.'[62] This is perhaps even surpassed by his
third: 'Apocalyptic forebodings aroused by the pace of change and the
vulnerability of a small world will concentrate minds on eternity.'[63]
Surely the Younger Berger is correct: 'There are many different theories of the roots of secularization, but whether one sees the process in
terms of the history of ideas (listing factors such as the growth of sci-

entific rationalism or the latent secularity of biblical religion itself), or whether one prefers more sociologically oriented theories (with factors such as industrialization, urbanization, or the pluralism of social milieux), it is difficult to see why any of these elements should suddenly reverse themselves.'[64]

Norris and Inglehart explain the decline of religion through a theory of 'existential security': as a society (or an individual) becomes more comfortable and secure and moves from fear of disaster and death to feelings of relative well-being, the demand for religion diminishes.[65] This idea that religion meets needs of human insecurity seems incontrovertible; recall William James: 'Here is the real core of the religious problem: Help! Help!'[66] Riesebrodt develops this idea, arguing that religion can be understood as 'a resource of cultural crisis prevention and management'. He argues that 'secularization has occurred as a consequence of increasing human control and "world-mastery" ... However, in part simultaneously, in part with some time lag, new dimensions of uncertainty, risk, and powerlessness have opened up.' Environmental catastrophe, nuclear war, the uncertainties and irrationalities of the market, the dissolution of kinship relations and the like 'have paved the way for a resurgence of religious modes of crisis prevention and management'. But Riesebrodt is speaking primarily of the South. To the extent that he has the West in mind, this seems incorrect. The new cognitive style has changed everything, leading to a sense of mastery of fate or the feeling that, given time and application, we will eventually solve our problems.[67] In Weber's famous words:

> The growing process of intellectualization and rationalization does *not* imply a growing understanding of the conditions under which we live. It means something quite different. It is the knowledge or the conviction that if *only we wished* to understand them we *could* do so at any time. It means that in principle, then, we are not ruled by mysterious, unpredictable forces, but that, on the contrary, we can in principle *control everything by means of calculation*. That in turn means the disenchantment of the world.[68]

Western fears, admittedly unprecedented, have warranted the negotiation of disarmament treaties, protocols on global warming, the establishment of the World Trade Organization and the International Criminal Court, but hardly a return to the supernatural.

The magnitude of the shift we have been describing escapes many. Brown and Woodhead's *That Was the Church That Was: How the Church of England Lost the English People*, provides a good example. They argue that the decline of the Church of England is its own fault. But to claim that had the Archbishops of Canterbury not been so stupid, each more stupid than his predecessor (the authors' language can be rather intemperate), the people of England would have remained happy with a worldview recognisably 'Anglican' is not serious. In Britain since the 1960s the supernatural has receded to the periphery in the lives of the majority. Christian churches were built on a supernatural worldview, a belief in a supreme God who became incarnate in Jesus, who has revealed his will through his anointed spokesmen who reveal the way to heaven or hell, who makes divine grace available through sacraments and whom we can influence through prayer. In the modern West, as I have argued, this otherworldly imagination has ceased to have its traditional purchase, so an institution built on that worldview has problems. Options open to it are fairly limited. So it is no more serious to suggest that the Church of England should re-identify with 'the people' by reinventing itself as provider of yoga, reflexology, tai chi, baby showers, high school proms, new rituals for disposing of funeral ashes and 'diverse forms of … non-religion'.[69] In dealing with the nation's *social* changes, these authors have almost nothing to say about the not unrelated but far more significant *change in consciousness* in Britain. What have disappeared are not just social institutions, but a previously almost pervasive worldview.

Flatt's treatment of the United Church of Canada provides a similar case. Up till the 1960s, the 'quiet modernism' of the leaders of the UCC was in tension with but coexisted with the 'loud evangelicalism' of conversion, crusades and public involvement. But in the 1960s, as a result of both worldwide factors and more local issues, the church formally adopted 'modernism', and virtually excluded Evangelicalism. The book traces this transformation, outlining the major steps on this trajectory (the new religious curriculum in particular, but other official statements, too). Flatt is convinced that the conscious opting for 'modernism' is the reason for the catastrophic decline in the membership: 'The numerical decline resulted from the actions taken by the church itself.'[70] Put another way, if they had remained true to their Evangelical roots, they would not have declined, or declined in anything like such numbers. This is seen, he claims, from the flourishing groups that continued to hold to their Evangelical heritage. But this argument seems perverse. The Evangelical groups that Flatt compares with the UCC are minuscule; in 2000 even the post-collapse UCC contains twice the numbers of Flatt's three Evangelical groups together.[71] Using Christian Smith's theory explaining the 'strength and persistence' of religious groups in a modern pluralistic society may help explain these small subcultural, even countercultural, sects, but it explains little about what has happened to Canadian culture generally.[72] The secularisation thesis, dismissed (ever so predictably and) too glibly here,[73] does: the education, affluence, mobility, independence and individualism of modern Canadians, their exposure to mass media, technology and commerce, and other aspects of modernity (unavoidable from the 1960s), have given them a new consciousness which makes problematic any simple appeal to traditional Christianity. It is not that the UCC authorities 'shot themselves in the proverbial feet' by renouncing their Evangelical roots.[74] The UCC, like the Church of England, relates closely to Canadian society; the church's fortunes illustrate the effects of recent cognitive (and, of course, social and cultural) changes on religion generally.

Many others seem to share the idea that if the churches could only get their act together and undo their mistakes, things would return to normal. For Steinfels, the Catholic Church needs correctives to 'postconciliar floundering'.[75] For Smith, too, the Catholic Church 'dropped the ball' after the Second Vatican Council, implying that a wiser course of action could have saved the day.[76] For McGrath, the decline and decay of the mainline churches is 'largely self-inflicted', principally by theologians and biblical critics.[77] The WCC and the ecumenical movement it represented were a disaster. Luckily, the Enlightenment is now 'defunct' and 'discredited and widely abandoned'.[78] The remedy, found mainly in the US, is postmodernism, understood as 'the total rejection of the leading ideas of the Enlightenment, including its demand that everything should be neatly ordered, rational and logical'.[79] This seems doubly perverse. What we have witnessed is the eclipse of the rationale of Christian churches traditionally understood.

The New Atheists equally miss the significance of the 'great ditch'. They have raised important issues, though they all ruin their case with a lack of historical awareness, denouncing believers of the past from the viewpoint of a consciousness arising only after 'the great ditch' and spreading generally only after the 1960s.[80]

One can doubt the effectiveness of the project of 'secularised' Christianity. We have noted Cupitt's argument that the secular West is Christianity in its modern form. Others have reformulated traditional Christianity in a way that is 'acceptable' today. But such contortions surely only provide a way for these particular authors to move graciously away from previous beliefs. Their chances of gathering adherents to their new secularised Christianity seem slight; above all, the appeal to a new generation seems doomed.[81]

Many of course lament the way things have turned out. Many insist that our modernity was not inevitable. One can admit this, but nevertheless answer that it has in fact occurred. Many lament (which is something different) that the modern world has brought problems on a scale hitherto unimaginable. One can admit, with Eagleton, that the Enlightenment has been 'at one and the same time an enthralling advance in humanity and an insupportable nightmare'.[82] We can lament the lost simplicities of the past; Bossy even seems to express a preference for the medieval over either the Reformation or Counter-Reformation world.[83] But there seems no way back to the comforts of an organic community and its reassuring cognitive style. Bruce reminds us, 'The fondness of politicians, social workers, and countercultural spiritualists for talking about community should not blind us to the fact that modernization has destroyed it.' For him, 'the two master trends of modernization', cultural diversity and individual autonomy, can only emphasise that it is we who choose our tradition, it is not the tradition that has created us. 'This is the cancer of choice.'[84] Berger too acknowledges that one can bemoan modern alienation, *anomie* and meaninglessness, but alienation is the precondition of both individuality and freedom, 'and *that* is not something I am willing to bemoan'.[85] Simply reading a newspaper shows that we have not succeeded in mastering the challenges that modernity poses; but it makes equally evident that the old answers are no longer viable or even particularly valued.

NOTES

PREFACE

1. *Standard*, 4 Sept. 2007, 6.
2. https://www.news24.com/Africa/News/rwanda-closes-thousands-of-churches-in-bid-for-more-control-20180404; accessed 14 Feb. 2019.

INTRODUCTION

1. J.D.Y. Peel, *Religious Encounter and the Making of the Yoruba*, Bloomington and Indianapolis: Indiana University Press, 2000, 216, emphasis in original.

1. ISSUES

1. Peter L. Berger, *Adventures of an Accidental Sociologist: How to Explain the World without Becoming a Bore*, Amherst: Prometheus Books, 2011, 94.
2. Martin Riesebrodt, *The Promise of Salvation: A Theory of Religion*, Chicago and London: University of Chicago Press, 2010, 74–6. Riesebrodt uses the term 'superhuman' rather than 'supernatural' since the concept of nature is a specifically modern one, which presupposes a law like the order of nature (ibid., 194). Riesebrodt is building on Spiro's definition, but expands Spiro's 'super-human beings' to include impersonal powers (Melford E. Spiro, 'Religion: Problems of Definition and Explanation', in Michael Banton (ed.), *Anthropological Approaches to the Study of Religion*, London: Tavistock, 1966, 85–126).
3. Charles Taylor, *A Secular Age*, Cambridge: Harvard University Press, 2007, 15; Steve Bruce, *Secularization: In Defence of an Unfashionable Theory*, OUP, 2001, 1; Peter L. Berger, *The Sacred Canopy: Elements of a Sociological Theory of Religion*, New York: Anchor Books, 1990 [1969],

Appendix 1, 175–7; David Martin, *A General Theory of Secularization*, Oxford: Blackwell, 1978, 12.

4. Cavanaugh's principal objection is that 'defining religion in terms of the transcendent or the sacred or the supernatural or the supra-empirical or any such terms just begs the question as to what those terms mean' (William Cavanaugh, *The Myth of Religious Violence*, New York: OUP, 2009, 105). That is far too strong. Berger admits the difficulties, but continues: 'Nevertheless, the term [viz supernatural], particularly in its everyday usage, denotes a fundamental category of religion, namely the assertion of belief that there is *an other reality*, and one of ultimate significance for man, which transcends the reality within which our everyday experience unfolds' (Peter L. Berger, *A Rumour of Angels: Modern Society and the Rediscovery of the Supernatural*, London: Penguin, 1970 [1969], 14, italics in original).

5. Thus Berger: definitions can be 'only more useful or less so. For this reason, it makes relatively little sense to argue over definitions … The only sensible attitude in matters of definition is one of relaxed tolerance … I am not at all interested in taking a doctrinaire position in favor of substantive definitions at all times and in all places, but only in defending the choice of a substantive definition here' (*Sacred Canopy*, 175). Bruce in another context has defended the position that 'some loose largely commonsensical conceptualization of religion is sufficient to allow us to get on with [the work in hand]' (Steve Bruce, 'Defining Religion: A Practical Response', *International Review of Sociology*, 21, 1 (2011), 118).

6. Ronald Dworkin, 'Religion without God', *NYRB*, 4 April 2013, 67–74.

7. James A. Beckford, *Religion and Advanced Industrial Society*, London: Routledge, 1989, 3–4.

8. James A. Beckford, *Social Theory and Religion*, CUP, 2003, 5.

9. Malory Nye, *Religion: The Basics*, London: Routledge, 2003.

10. Will Herberg, *Protestant-Catholic-Jew*, rev. edn, New York: Doubleday, 1960, 75.

11. Danièle Hervieu-Léger, *Religion as a Chain of Memory*, Cambridge: Polity, 2000 [1993].

12. Matthew Arnold, *St Paul and Protestantism*, [1870], vi, 33, cited in Stefan Collini, *Matthew Arnold: A Critical Portrait*, OUP, 1994, 96.

13. Terry Eagleton, *Culture and the Death of God*, New Haven and London: Yale University Press, 2015. Eagleton writes: 'The contemporary version of religion is sport. It is sport, with its sacred icons, revered traditions, symbolic solidarities, liturgical assemblies and pantheon of heroes, which is the opium of the people' (ibid., 45).

14. Linda Woodhead and Paul Heelas, *Religion in Modern Times*, Oxford: Blackwell, 2000, 9.

15. Hugh McLeod, *The Religious Crisis of the 1960s*, OUP, 2007, 18.

16. Kenneth L. Woodward, *Getting Religion: Faith, Culture and Politics from the Age of Eisenhower to the Era of Obama*, New York: Convergent, 2016, 96–7 (see also 98).

17. Ross Douthat, *Bad Religion: How We Became a Nation of Heretics*, New York: Free Press, 2012, 48 (also 275).

18. Diarmaid MacCulloch, 'Tidy-mindedness', *LRB*, 37, 18 (24 Sept. 2015), 17.

19. Cited in Nye, *Religion*, 16.

20. Cavanaugh, *Myth*, 9.

21. *Economist* News Desk, 6 Nov. 2017. Stark contrasts religion and spirituality, saying religion (or as he calls it, 'religiousness') should be understood as 'institutionalized beliefs and practices including church membership, church attendance and commitment to organizationally sanctioned doctrines'; so '"spirituality" is a form of "unchurched religion"', though to compound the confusion, 'spirituality without religion is not widespread and is not really irreligious' (Rodney Stark, *What Americans Really Believe*, Waco: Baylor University Press, 2008, 179). It is primarily Stark that Bruce had in mind when justifying his 'frustration with the malign influence of a small clique of US sociologists of religion' (Steve Bruce, *Choice and Religion: A Critique of Rational Choice*, OUP, 1999, 1).

22. Zadie Smith, 'On Optimism and Despair', address given in Berlin, 10 November 2016, on receiving Welt Literature Prize, in *NYRB*, 22 Dec. 2016.

23. The excessive singling out of religion is stressed very strongly by Elizabeth Shakman Hurd, *Beyond Religious Freedom: The New Global Politics of Religion*, Princeton: Princeton University Press, 2016.

24. Richard Dawkins, *A Devil's Chaplain*, London: Weidenfeld and Nicolson, 2003, 159; italics in original.

25. A.C. Grayling, *The Age of Genius: The Seventeenth Century and the Birth of the Modern Mind*, London: Bloomsbury, 2015.

26. Cavanaugh, *Myth*. He argues that those who persist in maintaining that it was a war of religion are perpetuating a myth whose function today is to suggest that religion (particularly of course Islam) is the cause of all violence and to divert attention from the violence done in the name of the secular nation state (particularly the US). Cavanaugh's treatment is primarily philosophical. For a detailed historical refutation of the 'religious' nature of the conflict, see Peter H. Wilson, *Europe's Tragedy: A New History of the Thirty Years War*, London: Penguin, 2015. Erdozain sees Cavanaugh's downplaying of the religious element simply as Christian special pleading (Dominic Erdozain, *Soul of Doubt:*

The Religious Roots of Unbelief from Luther to Marx, New York: OUP, 2016, 297).

27. David Martin, *Does Religion Cause War?*, OUP, 2004.

28. For a discussion of precisely this, see Philip L. Barnes, 'Was the Northern Ireland Conflict Religious?', *JCR*, 20 (2005), 55–69; Steve Bruce, 'Religion in the Northern Ireland Conflict', *Annali di storia dell'esegesi*, 26, 2 (2009), 301–23; Steve Bruce, *Paisley: Religion and Politics in Northern Ireland*, New York: OUP, 2007; John Fulton, 'Sociology, Religion and "The Troubles" in Northern Ireland: A Critical Approach', *Economic and Social Review*, 20 (1988), 5–24; John Fulton, 'Religion and Enmity in Ireland: Institutions and Relational Beliefs', *Social Compass*, 49 (2002), 189–202; John Fulton, *The Tragedy of Belief: Division, Politics, and Religion in Ireland*, OUP, 1991; Marianne Elliott, *When God Took Sides: Religion and Identity in Ireland*, OUP, 2009.

29. Nicholas Atkin and Frank Tallett, *Priests, Prelates and People: A History of European Catholicism since 1750*, New York: OUP, 2003, 25.

30. Fulton, *Tragedy*, esp. chs. 5–7.

31. Steve Bruce, 'Post-Secularity and Religion in Britain: An Empirical Assessment', *JCR*, 28 (2013), 368.

32. The 1999 British Methodist Conference's debate on letting people join their church without believing in God seems a perverse and doomed response to their decline (*Newsweek*, 12 July 1999, 50–5).

33. Berger, *Sacred Canopy*, Appendix 1, 175–7; Berger, *Adventures*, 94.

34. Berger, *Adventures*, 136–40. Giddens uses the same three factors to make exactly the same point, Anthony Giddens, *Sociology*, Cambridge: Polity Press, 2006, 569–71.

35. Richard Hoggart, *Uses of Literacy*, London: Penguin, 2009 [1957], 99 & 101.

36. Lexington, 'Donald Trump, Man of God', *Economist*, 20 May 2017, 40. The article continues that, seen that way, Evangelicalism is 'hard to untangle from other markers of conservative identity, from gun ownership to feeling the country is going to the dogs'.

37. Nick Spencer, 'David Cameron', in Nick Spencer (ed.), *The Mighty and the Almighty: How Political Leaders Do God*, London: Biteback Publishing, 2017, 281. Of course, this is the case not only in the West, as the chapter on Liberia's Ellen Johnson Sirleaf shows (167–78). In Liberia, Christian affirmations have always been an integral part of political discourse—with varying (or no) effects on the body politic (see Paul Gifford, *Christianity and Politics in Doe's Liberia*, CUP, 1993).

38. Joseph Ewing, 'Victor Orbán', in Spencer, *Mighty*, 117–25.

39. Hannah Malcolm, 'George W. Bush', in Spencer, *Mighty*, 149.

40. Nick Spencer, 'Conclusion', in Spencer, *Mighty*, 338.

41. See his 'Jesus', in Clive James, *A Point of View*, London: Picador, 2011, 217–22 (talk delivered BBC Four, 26 & 28 Dec. 2008).

42. Matthew Parris, 'As an Atheist, I Truly Believe Africa Needs God', *The Times*, 27 Dec. 2008.

43. Berger, *Rumour*, 28. Eagleton's claim that 'Christianity was never meant to be an *explanation* of anything', and to suppose it was is like thinking 'a novel is a botched piece of sociology' or ballet 'a botched attempt to run for a bus'—typical of his racy but frequently unhelpful reasoning (Terry Eagleton, *Reason, Faith and Revolution: Reflections on the God Debate*, New Haven: Yale University Press, 2009, 7 (italics in original), 6 & 50).

44. Bruce, *Secularization*, 37.

45. http://www.huffingtonpost.com/2013/07/23/most-religious-countries-least-religious_n_3640033.html; accessed 8 Aug. 2013.

46. David Aaronovitch, *Party Animals: My Family and Other Communists*, London: Vintage, 2017 [2016]. Thus a character in an early David Lodge novel in reference to the Trinity: 'In fact you don't really believe it, because your assent is never tested. Since it costs you nothing to accept the idea of three in one, you have never bothered to enquire why you *should* accept anything so utterly contrary to logic and experience' (*The British Museum Is Falling Down*, London: Penguin, 1983 [1965], 59).

47. Hal Lindsey with C.C. Carlson, *The Late Great Planet Earth*, New York: Bantam, 1970. Lindsey describes (with battle plans) the supposedly imminent World War Three, and claims to have lectured at the Pentagon (*Newsweek*, 5 Nov. 1984, 57).

48. Bryan Wilson, *Religion in Sociological Perspective*, Oxford: OUP, 1982, 176–7; also 43–4.

49. Ibid., 38.

50. David Martin, *The Education of David Martin*, London: SPCK, 2013, 139.

51. Hoggart, *Uses*, 98.

52. Probably in this case, he meant little more than belief in some form of afterlife (ibid., 96–7). Equally uninformative is McKibbin's reference to (in the 1930s) 'a marginal Christianity which is nonetheless strongly held' (Ross McKibbin, *Classes and Cultures: England 1918–1951*, New York: OUP, 1998, 290).

53. Tom Ingliss, 'Catholic Identity in Contemporary Ireland: Belief and Belonging to Tradition', *JCR*, 22 (2007), 205.

54. J.L. Houlden, *Bible and Belief*, London: SPCK, 1991, 79.

55. Spencer argues that in the few years before Britain's 2014 census the shift occurred: '"Christian" has become much a label of choice, "no

religion" increasingly becoming the default option' (Nick Spencer, *Doing Good: A Future for Christianity in the 21st Century*, London: Theos, 2016, 16).

56. C. Kirk Hadaway, Penny Long Marler and Mark Chaves, 'What the Polls Don't Show: A Closer Look at US Church Attendance', *American Sociological Review*, 58 (1993), 741–52; discussed in Robert Wuthnow, *Inventing American Religion: Polls, Surveys, and the Tenuous Quest for a Nation's Faith*, New York: OUP, 2015, 131–7.

57. David Voas, 'The Rise and Fall of Fuzzy Fidelity in Europe', *European Sociological Review*, 25, 2 (2009), 161.

58. Steve Bruce, *God Is Dead: Secularization in the West*, Oxford: Blackwell, 2002, 188.

59. Stark, *What Americans Really Believe*; questions respectively pages 26, 65, 179.

60. *Guardian*, 24 April 2000, 11. Sam Harris begins his tirade against religion with the claim that polls have shown that 53% of Americans are creationists, and 44% believe that Jesus will return some time in the next fifty years. His concern is unwarranted (Sam Harris, *Letter to a Christian Nation: A Challenge to Faith*, London: Bantam Press, 2007 [2006], xiv-xvi).

61. Nye, *Religion*, 63.

62. Berger, *Accidental*, 143; also 220.

63. The *Codex Calixtinus* or *Liber Sancti Jacobi* (https://codexcalixtinus.es/the-english-version). Book Five contains such unforgettable warnings as this of the Navarrese: 'Malicious, dark, hostile-looking types, crooked, perverse, treacherous, corrupt and untrustworthy, obsessed with sex and booze, steeped in violence, wild, savage, condemned and rejected, sour, horrible and squabbly. They are badness and nastiness personified.' Throw in their penchant for bestiality, and one can only conclude that 'they are descended from the Scots, because they have such similar customs' (ch. 7).

64. Other this-worldly aspects are suggested in another guidebook for pilgrims to the East. Arnold von Harff's fifteenth-century memoirs contain useful phrases in nine different languages: Croatian, Albanian, Greek, Arabic, Hebrew, Turkish, Hungarian, Basque and Breton. Thus, 'Wash my shirt for me—I do not understand—Will you sell me that?—How much is this?—Madam, shall I marry you?—Madam, shall I sleep with you?—Good woman, I am already in your bed' (cited in Jonathan Sumption, *Pilgrimage: An Image of Mediaeval Religion*, London: Faber and Faber, 1975, 195).

65. 'Compostelle n'est pas un pèlerinage chrétien … Il n'appartient en propre à aucun culte et, à vrai dire, on peut y mettre tout ce que

l'on souhaite. S'il devait être proche d'une religion, ce serait à la moins religieuse d'entre elles, celle qui ne dit rien de Dieu mais permet à l'être humain d'en approcher l'existence: Compostelle est un pèlerinage bouddhiste' (Jean-Christophe Rufin, *Immortelle randonnée. Compostelle malgré moi*, Paris: Gallimard, 2013, 181).

66. Shirley MacLaine, *The Camino: A Journey of the Spirit*, New York: Atria Books, 2000.

67. Grace Davie, with her expansive understanding of religion, simply describes pilgrimage as 'an increasingly popular form of religious life in modern Europe' (Davie, *Religion in Modern Europe: A Memory Mutates*, OUP, 2000, 150). For Davie, although Europe's historical churches may be declining, 'significant numbers of Europeans' ask questions about health, the purpose of existence and ecology, so religion is flourishing, if 'mutating' (ibid., 181). Obviously, her approach is of little relevance to my argument in this book.

68. Cited *Newsweek*, 16 Oct. 2015, 18.

69. Bernard Lewis (and Buntzie Ellis Churchill), *Notes on a Century: Reflections of a Middle East Historian*, London: Weidenfeld and Nicolson, 2012, 63–4.

70. *Economist*, 19 Nov. 2016, 11.

71. Ernest Gellner, 'The Importance of Being Modular', in John A. Hall (ed.), *Civil Society: Theory, History, Comparison*, Cambridge: Polity Press, 1995, 32–55.

72. David Voas and Steve Bruce, 'The 2001 Census and Christian Identification in Britain', *JCR*, 19 (2004), 27.

73. Ibid.

74. Ibid.

75. Ibid.

76. Ibid.

77. Beckford, *Religion and Advanced*, 46.

78. Wilfred Cantwell Smith, *What Is Scripture?*, London: SCM, 1989.

79. John Carey, *The Unexpected Professor: An Oxford Life in Books*, London: Faber and Faber, 2014, 187–8.

80. Harold Bloom, *The American Religion: The Emergence of the Post-Christian Nation*, New York: Simon and Schuster, 1992, 222. This is more fruitful approach to Evangelicals' use of the Bible than Bruce's asserting their 'empirical epistemological' mentality (Bruce, *God Is Dead*, 112–6).

81. James Tunstead Burtchaell, *The Dying of the Light: The Disengagement of Colleges and Universities from Their Christian Churches*, Grand Rapids: Eerdmans, 1998, 790.

82. Philip Jenkins, 'Christianity Moves South', in Frans Wijsen and Robert

Schreiter (eds), *Global Christianity: Contested Claims*, Amsterdam and New York: Rodophi, 2007, 19.

83. Berger, *Adventures*, 232.

84. Paul Gifford, 'A Contemporary Nigerian Reading of the Bible', *Journal of Theology for Southern Africa*, 152 (2015), 38–56; Paul Gifford, 'A Nigerian Reading of the Bible and Its Interpretational Power', in Klaus Hock (ed.), *The Power of Interpretation: Imagined Authenticity, Appropriated Identity: Conflicting Discourses on New Forms of African Christianity*, Wiesbaden: Harrassowitz Verlag, 2016, 25–37.

85. Stark, *What Americans Really Believe*, 34; see 95–100.

86. Steven Weinberg, *To Explain the World: The Discovery of Modern Science*, London: Penguin, 2016 [2015], 28.

87. Owen Chadwick, *The Secularization of the European Mind in the Nineteenth Century*, Oxford: OUP, 1975, 164.

88. Cavanaugh, *Myth*, 7.

89. Gerald Brenan, *The Spanish Labyrinth*, 2nd edn, CUP, 2014 [1950], 81.

90. Stefan Collini, 'What's Not to Like?', *LRB*, 2 June 2011, 10–12, a review of John A. Hall, *Ernest Gellner: An Intellectual Biography*, London: Verso, 2010.

91. Matthew Arnold, *The Complete Prose Works of Matthew Arnold*, ed. R.H. Super, Ann Arbor: University of Michigan Press, vol. 6, 168, cited in Collini, *Matthew Arnold*, 3–4.

2. A COGNITION TRANSFORMED

1. The paradigms are sketched on the endpapers of Hans Küng, *Christianity: The Religious Situation of our Time*, London: SCM, 1995 [German edn, 1994].

2. Dennis Nineham, *Christianity Mediaeval and Modern*, London: SCM, 1993, 84, to which I am heavily indebted here. For the persistence of medieval Catholicism into the modern world, see Owen Chadwick, *The Popes and European Revolution*, OUP, 1981, esp. 'The Religion of the People', 3–95.

3. Nineham, *Christianity*, 120.

4. Ibid., 31.

5. 'In this vale of tears, some pray, others fight, and still others work. The three groups are interconnected and cannot stand alone, so that the function of one group relies on the works of the other two, and in turn, all three ensure mutual assistance' (Adalberon, Bishop of Laon, about AD 1030, cited in Franco Cardini (translated by Corrado Federici), *The Companion to Medieval Society*, Montreal and Kingston: MQUP, 2012, 39). Essentially Gellner's producers, 'thugs' and 'humbugs',

or alternatively producers, 'sword-users' and 'script-users', performing respectively the tasks of production, coercion and legitimation: 'Thugs and priests between them inherit domination of the agrarian world' (Ernest Gellner, *Plough, Sword and Book: The Structure of Human History*, London: Collins Harvill, 1988; see 240, 94, 276).

6. Nineham, *Christianity*, 162.

7. R.H. Tawney, *The Agrarian Problem in the Sixteenth Century*, London: Longman, Green & Co., 1912, 64, cited in Nineham, *Christianity*, 251 n. 6, and see entire note for other estimates of medieval mobility.

8. Nineham, *Christianity*, 119–20.

9. Ibid., 164.

10. Ibid., 203.

11. Sumption, *Pilgrimage*, 100. Sumption's introduction contains the most disarming excuse—or non-excuse—for his biased selection of examples: 'I love France; German history bores me' (ibid., 10).

12. Ibid., 129 & 102.

13. 'The first crusade is the central event in the history of mediaeval Christianity ... [Yet] the crusading movement was ultimately to destroy the spiritual values of Christian Europe' (ibid., 137).

14. Ibid., 141.

15. Ibid., 295. 'During the twelfth century the papacy granted indulgences sparingly, and made only modest claims for them. Others, however, were less restrained ... Towards the end of the thirteenth century the papacy itself started to issue indulgences more generously. The indulgence which finally opened the floodgates was the indulgence of the Portiuncula' (ibid., 142). The Portiuncula was the chapel near Assisi where St Francis had died in 1226; the monks here claimed that Francis had obtained from the Pope a plenary indulgence, like that from crusading. Note that 'The laity accepted the efficacy of indulgences for the dead for many years before the popes granted them in formal terms' (ibid., 298). For the development of both indulgences and purgatory, see John Bossy, *Christianity in the West 1400–1700*, OUP, 1985, 54–6 & 30 respectively.

16. Nineham, *Christianity*, 231.

17. For example, Rodney Stark, 'Efforts to Christianize Europe 400–2000', *JCR*, 16 (2001), 105–23, where he argues that the secularisation thesis is incorrect because 'religious participation was never very high'.

18. Euan Cameron, *Enchanted Europe: Superstition, Reason, and Religion 1250–1750*, New York: OUP, 2010.

19. Sumption, *Pilgrimage*, 58; see also 44.

20. Steve Bruce, 'The Pervasive World View: Religion in Pre-Modern

Britain', *British Journal of Sociology*, 48, 4 (1997), 676–7. Bruce's conclusion: 'In concentrating on the extent to which the laity continued with pre-Christian practices and fell short of diligent conformity to the standards of the church, they fail to appreciate that the very same evidence shows a thoroughly supernaturalist view of the world. This is what is at the heart of the secularization thesis. What is required in the contrast between the past and the present is that there be an identifiable difference between then and now in the popularity and salience of *beliefs, actions and institutions which assume the existence of supernatural entities with powers of action or impersonal powers or processes possessed of moral purpose*' (ibid., 679, italics in original).

21. Eamon Duffy, quoted in Libby Purves, *Holy Smoke: Religion and Roots, a Personal Memoir*, London: Hodder and Stoughton, 1998, 178.

22. Emmanuel le Roy Ladurie, *Mountaillou: Cathars and Catholics in a French Village 1294–1324*, London: Penguin, 1980 [1978]. The Inquisition's interrogations convey little about hell and purgatory, the latter not yet widely accepted, and for Albigensians heaven became available only after the Last Judgement.

23. Sumption, *Pilgrimage*, 14.

24. Cited in William Rosen, *Justinian's Flea: Plague, Empire and the Birth of Europe*, London: Pimlico, 2008 [2006], 217. For the same understanding expressed by John of Ephesus, Evagrius Scholasticus and the Emperor Justinian himself, see ibid., 223, 252, 272.

25. Cited in Barbara Tuchman, *A Distant Mirror: The Calamitous 14th Century*, London: Macmillan, 1979 [1978], 104.

26. 'Nothing could be farther from our minds than to propose an "idealist" explanation of secularization' (Berger, *Sacred Canopy*, 30).

27. Steven Shapin, *The Scientific Revolution*, Chicago: University of Chicago Press, 1996.

28. 'In 1650 nobody quite knew how to study the physical world. By 1700 the idea that the study of the physical world is all about facts, experiments, evidence, theories and laws of nature had become well established. Later scientific revolutions have transformed our knowledge, but they have not melted down and recast our idea of science' (David Wootton, *The Invention of Science: A New History of the Scientific Revolution*, London: Allen Lane, 2015, 457).

29. Wootton, *Invention*, 531. 'Galileo sought whenever possible to present his new sciences as mathematical demonstrations, not empirical extrapolations. Within this tradition knowledge is primarily mental, conceptual, theoretical, and in the end, mathematical' (ibid., 321). And Galileo used only geometry; calculus, algebra, probability theory came later. Wootton's judgement is more nuanced that Gribbin's claim that

Galileo was the first scientist (John Gribbin, *Science: A History*, London: Penguin, 2003 [2002], 33, 72 & 91).

30. Joel Mokyr, *A Culture of Growth: The Origins of the Modern Economy*, Princeton: Princeton University Press, 2017, 80; though see Weinberg, 'Scientists in the seventeenth and eighteenth centuries would invoke Bacon as a counterweight to Plato and Aristotle, somewhat as an American politician might invoke Jefferson without ever having been influenced by anything Jefferson said and did' (Weinberg, *To Explain the World*, 202).

31. Wootton, *Invention*, 61–5. A similar idea is expressed in Whitehead's subsequent refinement: 'The greatest invention of the nineteenth century was the invention of the method of invention', in Alfred North Whitehead, *Science and the Modern World*, New York: Simon and Schuster, 1997 [1925], 96.

32. 'Over the course of the next fifty years or so [after the 1650s] the fact, which had previously existed in a sort of intellectual limbo where it could have only a ghostly existence as a "phenomenon", came to be the very foundation of all knowledge ... We now swim in a sea of facts and think that they are merely a recitation of the obvious. But in early-eighteenth century Italy, where scholasticism still dominated university teaching, there was nothing self evident about these new English values, just as the Declaration of Independence's claim that all men are created equal had once been anything but self-evident' (Wootton, *Invention*, 308–9).

33. Ibid., 137–8.

34. A major plank of Grayling's account: Grayling, *The Age of Genius*.

35. 'The Scientific Revolution was a single transformative process, the cumulative consequence, not of one sort of change repeated many times but of several distinct types of change overlapping and interlocking with each other ... Five fundamental changes thus interacted and interlocked in the course of the seventeenth century to produce modern science. Changes in the wider culture, in the availability of and attitude to evidence, in instrumentation, in scientific theories narrowly defined, and in the language of science and the community of language users all operated across different time-scales, and were driven by different, independent factors. But the cumulative effect was a fundamental transformation in the nature of our knowledge of the physical world, the invention of science ... But ... it is apparent that the new science was about one thing more than anything else, and that is the triumph of experience over philosophy' (Wootton, *Invention*, 566–7).

36. Mokyr, *Culture*, 319.

37. For a defence of the notion of progress in science, see Steven Weinberg, 'Eye on the Present: The Whig History of Science', *NYRB*, 17 Dec. 2015, 82–4.

38. Robert K. Merton, 'Science, Technology and Society in Seventeenth-Century England', *Osiris*, 4 (1938), 360–3.

39. Mokyr, *Culture*, 114. That the British and American Enlightenments were not anti-religious is one of the major themes of Gertrude Himmelfarb, *The Roads to Modernity: The British, French and American Enlightenments*, London: Vintage, 2008 [2004].

40. Compare Gellner's assertion that the Counter-Reformation 'sent half a continent to sleep for centuries' (*Plough*, 236) with Chadwick's: 'The two Congregations [of the Inquisition and of the Index] hampered the progress of thought less than they enraged individual scholars', Chadwick *The Popes and European Revolution*, 330.

41. Gellner, *Plough*, 105; David Landes, *The Wealth and Poverty of Nations: Why Some Are So Rich and Some So Poor*, London: Little, Brown, 1998, 177; Brad S. Gregory, *The Unintended Reformation: How a Religious Reformation Secularized Society*, Cambridge, MA: Belknap/Harvard, 2012, 241, 262, 269–70.

42. Wootton, *Invention*, 575–6. Hugh Trevor-Roper calls Weber's thesis 'a thesis of startling simplicity and—in my opinion—demonstrable error. But how much poorer our understanding of the Reformation, how much feebler our interest in it would be today, if that challenge had not been thrown down, and taken up' (Adam Sisman, *Hugh Trevor-Roper: The Biography*, London: Weidenfeld and Nicolson, 2010, 297).

43. Gellner, *Plough*, 184. Because Christianity contributed to this concept of a uniform, dismantlable, investigatable nature, Gellner can say that 'the church helped dig its own grave' (ibid., 167).

44. Francis Fukuyama, *The Origins of Political Order: From Prehuman Times to the French Revolution*, New York: Farrar, Straus and Giroux, 2011, 275. Fukuyama thus attributes Christianity's contribution less to beliefs than to the institutional forms Western Christianity took.

45. Gellner, *Plough*, 158–71; quotation from p. 170.

46. Gregory, *Unintended Reformation*, 63. For a sympathetic but critical evaluation of Gregory, see Eamon Duffy, 'Rites of Passage: How Historians Have Refashioned the Reformation', *TLS*, 10 Feb. 2017, 15–17. In my opinion, all the historians considered there, including Gregory, give too much importance to 'religion' (understood imprecisely) and not enough to the cognitive shift discussed here.

47. Gregory, *Unintended Reformation*, 380.

48. Ibid., 353.

49. Ibid., 358.

50. Martin, *The Education of David Martin*, 227.
51. R.G. Collingwood, *An Autobiography*, with new intro by Stephen Toulmin, OUP, 1978 [1939], 78.
52. Wootton, *Invention*, 579. He continues: 'And other cultures interested in understanding, predicting, or controlling natural phenomena (and all cultures must be interested in these activities) should be able to recognize the utility of our knowledge (or our maps, or of our weather forecasts), just as indigenous Americans could recognize the advantages of horses and guns for hunting buffaloes.'
53. Weinberg, *To Explain the World*, 28. Weinberg writes of the historical belief 'that scientific theories should ultimately be founded solely on reason. We have learned to give this up ... like me, most physicists today are resigned to the fact that we will always have to wonder why our deepest theories are not something different' (ibid., 247).
54. Ibid., 265.
55. Gellner, *Plough*, 136.
56. Weinberg, *To Explain the World*, 29. Eagleton gives an example of such a non-question: 'What is the taste of geometry?' (Terry Eagleton, *The Meaning of Life: A Very Short Introduction*, OUP, 2007, 1).
57. Lucien Goldmann, *The Philosophy of the Enlightenment*, London: Routledge, 1973, 55, cited in Eagleton, *Culture*, 7–8.
58. Eagleton, *Culture*, 196.
59. Peter L. Berger, Brigitte Berger and Hansfried Kellner, *The Homeless Mind: Modernization and Consciousness*, London: Penguin, 1974. Another quality of modernity discussed in *Homeless Mind* is the pluralisation of social life worlds, but the above is sufficient to make the relevant point here.
60. Gellner, *Plough*, 124.
61. H.L. Mencken, *A Mencken Chrestomathy*, New York: Vintage, 1982, 13.
62. Richard Davenport-Hines (ed.), *Letters from Oxford: Hugh Trevor-Roper to Bernard Berenson*, London: Phoenix, 2006, xiii.
63. A.J. Ayer, *Part of My Life*, London: Collins, 1977, 156.
64. *Economist*, 5 Jan. 2002, 12.
65. Bruce, *God Is Dead*, 106–17.
66. Darren Oldridge, *The Supernatural in Tudor and Stuart England*, London: Routledge, 2016, 42.
67. Bruce, *Secularization*, 44.
68. Weinberg, 'Eye on the Present', 82.
69. Paul Gifford, *Christianity, Development and Modernity in Africa*, London: Hurst, 2015, 13–68.
70. G. Lienhardt, *Divinity and Experience: The Religion of the Dinka*, OUP, 1961.

71. Such a religion is aptly described as a 'mythic matrix', found universally 'if one goes back far enough in the religious history of every human culture' (Peter L. Berger, *Questions of Faith: A Skeptical Affirmation of Christianity*, Oxford: Blackwell, 2004, 22; see also ibid., 23–4, 43–4, 46–7).

72. *Walfadjri*, 7 March 2013, 6. A hundred and fifty civil society organisations from 29 African countries gathered in Dar es Salaam in June 2016 to address the issue; a Canadian charity documented 457 attacks on albinos, including 178 murders, in 26 African countries over the previous decade (Ethiopia's *Daily Monitor*, 21 June 2016, 4). Malawi's president reported 65 attacks on albinos in the previous 18 months (*Daily Monitor*, 2 June 1016, 7), and murders of at least five alleged vampires in October 2017 (*Daily Monitor*, 12 Oct. 2017, 7). A Catholic priest was arrested on suspicion of murdering an albino in Malawi in 2018 (*CISA*, 312, 22 May 2018). Attacks on bald men were reported in Mozambique in July 2017 (*Daily Monitor*, 5 July 2017, 7). Six Tanzanian children were reported killed 'for body parts' in early 2019 (*Daily Monitor*, 30 Jan. 2019, 7). A report on these issues was presented to the UN Human Rights Council on 23 Jan. 2018; see 'Report on the enjoyment of human rights by persons with albinism on the expert workshop on witchcraft and human rights', found at A/HRC/37/57Add2.

73. *Walfadjri*, 27 March 2013, 4.

74. *Quotidien*, 13 Feb. 2012, 9; *Populaire*, 10 Feb. 2012, 11; *Populaire*, 11/12 Feb. 2012, 10; *Populaire*, 13 Feb. 2012, 2; *Walfadjri*, 16 Feb. 2012, 6 & 12; *Observateur*, 17 Feb. 2012, 4; *Quotidien*, 18/19 Feb. 2012, 7–9; *Quotidien*, 23 Feb. 2012, 7; *Walfadjri*, 25/26 Feb. 2012, 7; *Gazette*, 23 Feb.—1 March 2012, 31–3.

75. *Observateur*, 18 Dec. 2012, 8. Ritual murders were reported in Liberia in October–November 2015, Uganda in March 2016, Zambia in April 2016, Nigeria in November 2017.

76. UNICEF, *Children Accused of Witchcraft: An Anthropological Study of Contemporary Practices in Africa*, Dakar: UNICEF/WCARO, 2010, 39–40.

77. For more detail, see Paul Gifford, 'Religion in Contemporary Senegal', *JCR*, 31, 2 (2016), 255–67; for this study I owe a considerable debt to Ibrahima Sow, *Divination, marabout, destin. Aux sources de l'imaginaire*, Dakar: IFAN Cheikh Anta Diop, 2009; Ibrahima Sow, *Le Maraboutage au Sénégal*, Dakar: IFAN Cheikh Anta Diop, 2013.

78. The subject of Ousmane Sembene's most famous film, *Xala*, for which see Richard Fardon and Senga la Rouge, *Learning from the Curse: Sembene's Xala*, London: Hurst, 2017.

79. *Observateur*, 5 June 2013, 16. He had paid 30 million fcfa for a previous bout against the then-champion Yekini.
80. Memory Mucherahowa, something of a football legend, revealed the extent of traditional healers' involvement in Zimbabwean football in his autobiography, *Soul of Seven Million Dreams* (CreateSpace Publishing, 2017), even advocating the (extremely dysfunctional) *juju* of slitting players' toes before a game. For a detailed treatment of the enchanted imagination in African football, see *African Soccer*, Aug.–Sept. 2001, 14–21.
81. Sow, *Maraboutage*, 365.
82. *Populaire*, 24/25 Dec. 2012, 13.

3. WESTERN RELIGION TODAY

1. Grace Davie, *Religion in Britain since 1945: Believing without Belonging*, Oxford: Blackwell, 1994.
2. Steve Bruce, 'Praying Alone? Church-going in Britain and the Putnam Thesis', *JCR*, 17, 3 (2002), 317–28. Grace Davie, 'A Reply to Steve Bruce', *JCR*, 17, 3 (2002), 329–34; Robert D. Putnam, *Bowling Alone: The Collapse and Revival of American Community*, New York: Simon and Schuster, 2000.
3. Davie, *Religion in Modern Europe*, 78–81.
4. Steve Bruce and David Voas, 'Vicarious Religion: An Examination and Critique', *JCR*, 25, 2 (2010), 243–59. Grace Davie responds in 'Vicarious Religion: A Response', *JCR*, 25, 2 (2010), 261–6. I have referred above to Hugh Trevor-Roper, Regius Professor of Modern History at Oxford. Attending a memorial service for one who would have disagreed with everything said, he lamented 'that this ridiculous mummery and mumbo-jumbo' should be the only way we know of paying tribute to the dead. 'To think also that such a farce may be performed over myself, that one day some old gaffer may intone to a skeptical congregation that I am now seeing my Creator face to face, & similar undiluted rubbish.' He consoled himself by reflecting on the advantage of set prayers, 'which is that no one need pay any attention to their meaning, or associate himself with the meaning of his own utterances' (Sisman, *Hugh Trevor-Roper*, 71).
5. Steve Bruce, 'Secularization: The Impotence of Individualized Religion', *The Hedgehog Review: After Secularization*, 8 (2006), 40–2. Bruce has supplementary data from the 2001 Scottish Social Attitudes survey, which indicate that 8% see divination as in any way important in their lives, 10% understand yoga or meditation in this way, and 20% alternative medicine. Above all, he finds 70% have never tried divination, 78% never tried yoga or meditation, and 55% alternative medicine (ibid., 40).

6. I find merely confusing Bruce's remark: 'Though many would initially avoid the religious tag, most human potential organizations do have at their core explicitly religious propositions. Heelas calls them "self-religions" because, if nothing else, their claim that the self is perfectible is a religious one' (*Choice*, 160). The claim that the self is perfectible is not necessarily or exclusively religious.

7. This point is well made by Bruce who argues that 'The Easternisation of the West' should really be phrased 'The Westernisation of the Easternisation of the West' (*God is Dead*, 118–39).

8. Woodward, *Getting Religion*, 290.

9. Ibid., 293.

10. Bloom, *American Religion*, 52.

11. Ibid., 186.

12. Ibid., 184–5. A point well made by Alan Wolfe, *The Transformation of American Religion*, New York: Fourth Estate, 2003.

13. Bruce, *Secularization*, 155.

14. Larry Siedentop, *Inventing the Individual: The Origins of Western Liberalism*, London: Penguin 2015 [2014].

15. Ibid., 188.

16. Ibid., 217.

17. Ibid., 253.

18. Ibid., 361.

19. Ibid., 292.

20. Nick Spencer, *The Evolution of the West: How Christianity Has Shaped Our Values*, London: SPCK, 2016. His chapters on Darwin, Charles Taylor (secularism) and Piketty (inequality) are less integrated into the overall argument.

21. Ibid., 127, 137. Tyndale, for one, would have been appalled with what his ideas led to.

22. Ibid., 143–4.

23. Ibid., 137. Rupert Shortt (*TLS*, 16 Dec. 2016, 3–5) in his review of *Evolution* imputes to Spencer what Spencer leaves most often implicit: 'Christianity, having created the modern world, also has the resources to cast necessary judgement on it and take it forward.' Hobson seems to hold that humanism is based on Christianity, and needs Christianity not just to be effective but to persist, even if this Christianity is expressed in 'post-religious terms'. Such wording contributes little to my argument here, and, indeed, for all the insight into thinkers as diverse as Rousseau, Mill and Nietzsche, Hobson seems to mean by Christianity little more than ritually celebrated doubt (Theo Hobson, *God Created Humanism: The Christian Basis of Secular Values*, London: SPCK, 2017, esp. 168, 173, 183).

24. Spencer, *Evolution*, 10. See also 149 & 184.
25. Ibid., 147. The confusion is increased when he uses the phrases 'spiritual but not religious' and 'religiosity shorn of God' without explaining how we might understand them.
26. Siedentop, *Inventing*, 360.
27. Cupitt singles out elements of Christianity that 'gave rise' to the modern West: God's emptying himself, identifying with humanity; the critical examination and purging that the monk in his cell directed *against himself* became (when objectified socially) the spirit of critical examination of modern Western thought; critical thinking, which is the child of the ancient polemic against idols; the negation of images; and the *via negativa* of Christian spirituality. The idea of 'the sacred' is gone. The 'death of God' occurred about AD 1720. Already by Jane Austen's time, supernatural, dogmatic Christianity was passé. 'The British Labour Party ... has done far more to build the Kingdom of God on earth during the past hundred years than the Latin Church achieved in the same territory during the whole millennium AD 600–1600' (Don Cupitt, *The Meaning of the West: An Apologia for Secular Christianity*, London: SCM, 2008, 154).
28. Ibid., 6.
29. Ibid., 34. Again, 'Western culture is Christianity objectified and secularized' (ibid., 55). The Church 'has been superseded by something bigger than itself, namely "the West", which is simply radical Christian humanism, and a lot closer to Jesus than the Church ever was' (ibid., 120).
30. Erdozain, *The Soul of Doubt*, 2.
31. Ibid., 175.
32. Ibid., 2.
33. Ibid., 6–7. Also: 'Modernity is a war of religious ideas, not a war on them' (ibid., 261). 'The "warfare" of science against religion ... was a religious phenomenon itself' (ibid., 182).
34. It may well be that Feuerbach's 'prophetic atheism was nothing less than "the necessary, irrepressible, irrefragable result of Christianity"' (ibid., 245, citing Feuerbach himself), and that Marx's 'materialist project was one of the more remarkable fruits of the accusing conscience' (ibid., 247), but it is totally confusing to characterise Marx as religious, or to claim of the 1848 Communist Manifesto: 'The indignation remains theological' (ibid., 259).
35. Ibid., 5.
36. Berger, *Sacred Canopy*, 107.
37. Chadwick, *Secularization*, 184.
38. See his encomium for Keble, John Henry Newman, *Apologia pro Vita Sua*, London: Penguin, 1994 [1864], 255–7.

39. Ibid., 458–73.
40. Ibid., see also 252–62.
41. Ibid., 235–7.
42. G.M. Young, *Portrait of an Age*, London: Phoenix Press, 2002 [1936], 76.
43. Mrs Humphry Ward, *Robert Elsmere*, OUP, 1987 [1888]. See also John Sutherland, *Mrs Humphry Ward: Eminent Victorian, Pre-eminent Edwardian*, OUP, 1990. For an overview of the literary context, see Robert Lee Wolff, *Gains and Losses: Novels of Faith and Doubt in Victorian England*, New York: Garland Publishing, 1977.
44. He continues: 'I grew up in a negative state with regard to it. I looked on the modern exactly as I did upon the ancient religion, as something which in no way concerned me' (John Stuart Mill, *The Autobiography*, ReadaClassic, 2010 [1873], 22).
45. Young, *Portrait*, 125.
46. 'There are times when the reader of Victorian apologetic, whether the theme be miracles or inspiration or the authorship of the gospels … is nauseated by the taint of sophistry and false scholarship, and feels, as the better intelligence of the time did feel, that if men could force their intellects to think like that, it cannot matter much what they thought' (Young, *Portrait*, 116). Chadwick notes the perception of the Christian churches as immoral (especially the Catholic Church with the likes of the *Syllabus of Errors*) because opposing justice and freedom (Chadwick, *Secularization*, 155).
47. See Timothy J. Madigan, *W.K. Clifford and 'The Ethics of Belief'*, Newcastle: Cambridge Scholars Publishing, 2009. The issues are brilliantly caught by Van A. Harvey in his two articles, 'Is There an Ethics of Belief?', *Journal of Religion*, 49, 1 (1969), 41–58, and 'The Ethics of Belief Reconsidered', *Journal of Religion*, 59, 4 (1979), 406–20. In the earlier article, he argues that one has no more right to a belief that he cannot defend than to a pint of beer for which he cannot pay; his rethinking a decade later claims that this was too stringent, and argues instead for 'responsible belief'.
48. Young, *Portrait*, 157.
49. Callum G. Brown, *The Death of Christian Britain*, London: Routledge, 2001; Callum G. Brown, *Religion and Society in Twentieth Century Britain*, Harlow: Pearson, 2006.
50. Alasdair Crockett and David Voas, 'Generations of Decline: Religious Change in Twentieth Century Britain', *Journal for the Scientific Study of Religion*, 45, 4 (2006), 567–84.
51. Steve Bruce and Tony Glendenning, 'When Was Secularization? Dating the Decline of the British Churches and Locating Its Cause', *British Journal of Sociology*, 61, 1 (2010), 107–26.

52. McLeod, *Religious Crisis*, 18.

53. In his chapter on counterculture he seems to think that the mind-expanding drug-taking culture of California constitutes a religious change (ibid., 124–40). Data about 'religious books as a proportion of all books published' convey little without knowing whether he is including categories like 'mind, body, spirit', 'self-help', 'alternative healing', 'meditation', 'New Age', 'astrology' and 'yoga' under the umbrella of religion (ibid., 61). He is undoubtedly correct in saying that churches, mosques and temples 'continue to be among the most significant institutions in [European] countries' (ibid., 254), but some attempt to differentiate the social and cultural from anything particularly religious is necessary.

54. Revealingly, McLeod in another study remarks on the lack of historical work on Christianity post-1945: 'There are many valuable studies by sociologists of contemporary religion, but, from a historian's point of view, their concern with identifying and interpreting overall trends leads them to neglect specific people, places and events, and the precise sequence of events' (Hugh McLeod, *Religion and the People of Western Europe 1789–1989*, new edn, OUP, 1997, 172). This comment can be turned on its head; abundance of historical details can preclude identifying overall trends.

55. Berger, *Sacred Canopy*, 166–7.

56. I would argue that theologians as diverse as Harry Williams (see his *True Resurrection*, London: Collins, 1983 [1972]), Gregory Baum (see his *The Social Imperative: Essays on the Critical Issues That Confront the Christian Churches*, New York: Paulist, 1979), even Avery Dulles (*Models of the Church*, New York: Random House, 1974), can be seen in this light. When the idea of 'models' is applied to Jesus, so that 'Son of God' becomes just one among others like 'Man for Others' and 'Prophet' etc., the conclusion is inescapable (John F. O'Grady, *Models of Jesus Revisited*, New York: Paulist, 1994).

57. A point missed by McLeod, *Religious Crisis*, in his discussion of Robinson.

58. David Lodge, *How Far Can You Go?*, London: Penguin, 1981 [1980].

59. Wilfred Sheed, *Essays in Disguise*, New York: Alfred A. Knopf, 1990, 111. A serious problem with Mark S. Massa, *The American Catholic Revolution: How the Sixties Changed the Church Forever*, New York: OUP, 2010, is that he is never clear whether the changes constituted a revolution or a reaction.

60. John W. O'Malley, *What Happened at Vatican II?*, Cambridge, MA: Harvard University Press, 2008, 15–52; 290–313.

61. Ibid., 89–91, 297.

62. Ibid., 89, 302.
63. Ibid., 291, 86, 84, 81.
64. O'Malley revealingly states that 'for Americans today, the declaration in the final form approved by the council reads almost like a statement of the obvious', because such principles 'have been operative in the United States since the ratification of the Constitution' (ibid., 212).
65. Ibid., 217. This shift was so dramatic that Archbishop Marcel Lefebvre, the future schismatic, 'predicted ruin for the Catholic Church if the declaration were adopted' (ibid.).
66. John W. O'Malley, *Trent: What Happened at the Council*, Cambridge, MA: Belknap/Harvard, 2013, 267–75.
67. The word 'liberation' first appeared in a papal document in Paul VI's *Evangelii nuntiandi* in 1975.
68. Eugene Carson Blake, 'Report', in Norman Goodall (ed.), *The Uppsala Report 1968: Official Report of the Fourth Assembly of the World Council of Churches, Uppsala, July 4–20 1968*, Geneva: WCC, 1968, 285–93. Two other observations of Blake's are of importance for my argument here. First, 'The God to whom we profess obedience is acting in this world and often through men and movements who do not know that they are serving him'. Second, his contrasting 'our world with that known by our ancestors since history began' (ibid.).
69. The section on Justice and Peace led the following year to the WCC's Programme to Combat Racism, controversial in that it gave money (eventually nearly US$10 million) to liberation movements like the ANC in South Africa, Unita and MPLA in Angola, Frelimo in Mozambique.
70. John Weller, 'Personal Comment', in Goodall (ed.), *Uppsala Report*, 20.
71. David L. Edwards, 'Personal Comment', in Goodall (ed.), *Uppsala Report*, 84.
72. Norman Goodall, 'Editorial', in Goodall (ed.), *Uppsala Report*, xvii.
73. O'Malley, *What Happened at Vatican II*, 280–2. For the development of indulgences, see Sumption, *Pilgrimage*, esp. 141–5, 230–42, 291.
74. *Tablet*, 2 June 2018, 27.
75. Cited in Nineham, *Christianity*, 80.
76. So Hayden's description of the Coutances Cathedral today: 'The once proudly displayed relics are discretely stored in a cabinet in the southern transept' (J. Michael Hayden, *The Catholicisms of Coutances: Varieties of Religion in Early Modern France 1350–1789*, Montreal and Kingston: MQUP, 2013, 103). Hayden's fine study, despite his avowed aim, is concerned primarily with practices and structures, not beliefs (ibid., 4). Relics have come to be everywhere downplayed, despite the relics of

Thérèse of Lisieux touring 40 countries in the last two decades, and the arm of St Francis Xavier touring 14 Canadian cities in early 2018. It is of interest here that Cardinal Basil Hume, Archbishop of Westminster, blocked Thérèse's relics coming to Britain in the late 1990s, probably because 'the veneration of relics was precisely the sort of traditional "peasant" Catholicism he had spent years spurning, in an effort to dispel any remaining suspicions that Catholicism was odd or foreign in its practices and so move it into the mainstream of national life' (Peter Stanford, 'Story of a Soul: Relics of Thérèse', *Standpoint*, September 2009, 32). John Thavis documents the enormous ambivalence in Rome to miracle claims, supposed apparitions and cases of possession. Aware of modern Western sensibilities, there is a reluctance officially to endorse such things, and great effort to control them. Thavis largely ignores the 'enchanted religious imagination' beyond the West. John Thavis, *The Vatican Prophecies: Investigating Supernatural Signs, Apparitions, and Miracles in the Modern Age*, New York: Viking, 2015.

77. Chadwick presents confession as virtually the centre of the clergy's ministry up till the nineteenth century; see *Popes and European Revolution*, 166.
78. Keith Thomas, *Religion and the Decline of Magic*, London: Penguin, 1973, 43.
79. Stark, *What Americans* Really *Believe*, 9.
80. Lyndal Roper, *Martin Luther: Renegade and Prophet*, London: Vintage, 2017 [2016], 354–5.
81. A poll before a Eucharistic Congress in Ireland found that only a quarter of Catholics polled believed the consecrated bread and wine become the body and blood of Christ at Mass (*Tablet*, 9 June 2012, 32).
82. David Hare, *Asking Around*, London: Faber and Faber, 1993, 5–6. For 'atheist vicars', see also Kirsty Milne, 'God in the Dock', *New Statesman and Society*, 1 April 1994, 16–18.
83. Laraine Fergenson, 'The Church: For Better and for Worse', *NYRB*, 20 April 2017, 65.
84. Such was obviously not the case for Dorothy Day, one of the most prominent activists, for whom love of God always manifestly drove love of neighbour; see Dorothy Day, *The Long Loneliness*, New York: HarperCollins, 1997 [1952], *passim*.
85. Douthat, *Bad Religion*, 100.
86. Owen Chadwick, *A History of the Popes 1830–1914*, OUP, 1998, 520.
87. Interview in *La Repubblica*, 19 Nov. 2004. Pope Benedict deplored the presence of secularisation 'within the very bosom of the Church', with

its superficiality, egocentrism, plummeting birth rates, moral relativism, inability to make lifelong commitments, rejection of the church's magisterium, surrogate forms of religious affiliation and vague spiritualism (*Tablet*, 15 March 2008, 31), and compared the contemporary situation to the decline of the Roman Empire (*Tablet*, 1 Jan. 2011, 31); the Vatican Secretary of State called the Irish referendum on gay marriage a 'defeat for humanity' (*Tablet*, 30 May 2015, 27).

88. And fierce criticism, like this from Australian theologian Anna Silvas: 'All too often we are subjected to long tracts of homespun avuncular advice that could be given by any secular journalist without the faith, the sort of thing to be found in the pages of *Reader's Digest*' (from address in July 2016 found on www.chiesa.expressonline.it; accessed 12 Dec. 2017).

89. Thomas Sheehan, 'Revolution in the Church', *NYRB*, 14 June 1984, 35–9; Hans Küng, *Eternal Life?*, London: HarperCollins, 1984. This debate was carried further by various authors in *Commonweal*, 10 Aug. 1984; 21 Sept. 1984; 5 Oct. 1984, and by Gerald O'Collins in *Tablet*, 13 Oct. 1984 and 20 Oct. 1984.

90. Michael Dummett, 'A Remarkable Consensus', *New Blackfriars*, 68 (1987), 424–31. For much the same argued by another British Catholic philosopher, see Hugo Meynell, 'Rahner's *Grundkurs* Revisited Again', *New Blackfriars*, 61 (July–Aug. 1980), where he writes: 'What many would maintain to be the assured results of modern New Testament scholarship are not compatible with Catholic or indeed any traditional Christian dogma. I do not think that one can say very much useful about the doctrinal disputes at present agitating the Church unless one grasps this point' (349).

91. Michael Dummett, 'Unsafe Premises: A Reply to Nicholas Lash', *New Blackfriars*, 68 (1987), 558–66. Lash's criticism of Dummett is found in Nicholas Lash, 'A Leaky Sort of Thing? The Divisiveness of Michael Dummett', *New Blackfriars*, 68 (1987), 552–7.

92. David Lodge, *Paradise News*, London: Penguin, 1992, 252–3.

93. Carl Braaten, 'An Open Letter to Bishop Mark Hanson', 11 July 2005, http://wordalone.org/docs/wa-braaten.shtml.

94. Spencer, *Doing Good*, 24; see also 17.

95. Ibid., 34.

96. Ibid., 55.

97. Ibid., 66.

4. US EXCEPTIONALISM

1. Bruce, *God Is Dead*, 204.

2. Peter Berger, Grace Davie and Effie Fokas, *Religious America, Secular Europe? A Theme and Variations*, Aldershot: Ashgate, 2008. Any claim of American exceptionalism is comprehensively refuted in David Voas and Mark Chaves, 'Is the United Sates a Counterexample to the Secularization Thesis?', *American Journal of Sociology*, 121, 5 (2016), 1517–56.

3. Thomas Albert Howard, *God and the Atlantic: America, Europe and the Religious Divide*, New York: OUP, 2011, 9–10. His referents for his second meaning are 'various forms of evangelical Protestantism, *the* juggernaut force in the nineteenth century, while also connoting the broader political-legal context of church disestablishment and religious voluntarism, which affected other forms of religious expression (Catholic, Jewish, Unitarian, Mormon, Deist) extensively'.

4. Berger et al., *Religious America*, 21. Mencken expresses the same point with characteristic élan: Episcopalians 'in most American cities are largely ex-Methodists or ex-Presbyterians, or in New York, ex-Jews' ('The Collapse of Protestantism', in Mencken, *Chrestomathy*, 78).

5. Woodward, *Getting Religion*, 48.

6. The National Center for Science Education in California reported in 2007 that in the previous five years, anti-evolution legislation had been introduced in 24 state legislatures and similar policies were under consideration in at least 20 states (*Guardian*, 15 Feb. 2007, 18).

7. *Los Angeles Times*, 16 June 1990, F12.

8. There are some like the Christian Reconstructionists associated with the likes of R.J. Rushdoony who do seem to want to reconfigure American society along biblical lines, up to and including stoning for adultery, but their significance is negligible.

9. For the origins and transformation of this movement, see George M. Marsden, *Fundamentalism and American Culture: The Shaping of Twentieth-Century Evangelicalism 1870–1925*, New York: OUP, 1980; Joel A. Carpenter, *Revive Us Again: The Reawakening of American Fundamentalism*, New York: OUP, 1997; and more recently Frances Fitzgerald, *The Evangelicals: The Struggle to Shape America*, New York: Simon and Schuster, 2017. For a sociological assessment of the contemporary scene, see Christian Smith, *American Evangelicalism: Embattled and Thriving*, Chicago: University of Chicago Press, 1998.

10. Leslie Griffiths, 'The Evangelist Who Played Golf with Presidents', *Tablet*, 14 June 1997, 733; he accuses Graham of effectively wedding his message 'to the interests of the ruling group of the day'. 'Just as I am' was the signature tune of Graham's crusades, sung at the altar-call by George Beverly Shea (linked to Graham as closely as Sankey to Moody). The 'grandly misnamed' is from Woodward, *Getting Religion*, 138.

11. Wuthnow, *Inventing American Religion*, 200.
12. Sarah Posner, 'Amazing Disgrace: How Did Donald Trump—a Thrice-Married Biblically Illiterate Sexual Predator—Hijack the Religious Right?', *New Republic*, 20 March 2017. Bruce accuses Stark of a 'naivety about race' (*Choice*, 126), a charge that could be levelled more widely.
13. Randall Balmer is cited, in connection with the 2017 candidacy of Judge Moore in Alabama, a candidacy mired in accusations of sexual impropriety and supported by evangelicals like Jerry Falwell Jr and Franklin Graham: 'In this case you have a movement that has so totally embraced a particular political party that it's willing to go along with any outrage as long as it's within the tent of the party' (Anstead W. Herndon, 'Why Evangelicals Are Again Backing a Republican despite Allegations of Sexual Misconduct', *Boston Globe*, 20 Nov. 2017).
14. See the discussions in Woodward, *Getting Religion*, 377–94; and Peter Steinfels, *A People Adrift: The Crisis of the Roman Catholic Church in America*, New York: Simon and Schuster, 2003, 85–102.
15. 'More Cracks in the Golden Dome', *National Review Online*, posted 14 June 2011, his italics; again: 'Pro life activism [is] *the* cultural marker of serious Catholicism in America' ('The End of the Bernardin Era: The Rise, Dominance and Fall of a Culturally Accommodating Catholicism', in *First Things*, Feb. 2011). And again: 'The pro-life cause [is] *the* cultural marker of serious Catholicism in America' ('Rose DeLauro, CNS and the Disoriented Catholic Left', EPPC newsletter posted 2 May 2012).
16. Steinfels, *People Adrift*, 95–6 for polling on American lay Catholic nuanced attitudes to abortion. Hoge shows only 31% of Catholics polled thought Catholic teaching opposing abortion was essential (Dean R. Hoge, 'Core and Periphery in American Catholic Teaching', *JCR*, 17 (2002), 293–302). The British liberal Catholic *Tablet* has queried the absolutist Catholic stance: thus Clifford Longley: 'A newly fertilised embryo is not, in any common sense view, a "person" as you and I' (*Tablet*, 19–26 Aug. 2017; also editorial, 16 Sept. 2017, 2); and see poll suggesting 'dramatic increase in Catholic acceptance of [some forms of] abortion from 33% in 1985 to 61% in 2016' (*Tablet*, 16 Sept. 2017, 28).
17. Damon Linker, *The Theocons: Secular America under Siege*, New York: Anchor Books, 2006, 74–6.
18. Michael Novak, 'A Papal Message Lost and Found', *San Francisco Times*, 24 Feb. 1988, 7.
19. *Tablet*, 11 July 2009, 5.
20. Reported in *Tablet*, 5 Sept. 2009, 31.

21. George Weigel, 'The Pope's Encyclical, at Heart, Is about *Us*, Not Trees and Snail Darters', *National Review Online*, 18 June 2015, reprinted in *Ethics and Public Policy Center newsletter*, accessed 21 July 2016.

22. Will Herberg, *Protestant-Catholic-Jew*, 74–5.

23. William E. Connolly, *Capitalism, Christianity, American Style*, Durham: Duke University Press, 2008, 2.

24. Ibid., 40; his emphasis.

25. Ibid., 39.

26. José Casanova, 'Rethinking Secularization: A Global Comparative Perspective', *The Hedgehog Review: After Secularization*, 8 (2006), 17.

27. 'Between them, Darwin and Spencer exercised such sovereignty over America as George III had never enjoyed' (H.S. Commager, *The American Mind: An Interpretation of American Thought and Character since the 1880s*, New Haven: Yale University Press, 1950, 87).

28. John Kenneth Galbraith, *The Age of Uncertainty*, London: BBC–André Deutsch, 1977, 44–5.

29. Commager, *American Mind*, 90.

30. Cited in Richard Hofstadter, *Social Darwinism in American Thought 1850–1915*, Philadelphia: University of Pennsylvania Press, 1945, 31.

31. Cited in Paul F. Boller Jr, *American Thought in Transition: The Impact of Evolutionary Naturalism, 1865–1900*, Chicago: Rand McNally, 1969, 55.

32. Ibid., 56.

33. For Beecher, see Galbraith, *Age of Uncertainty*, 49–50.

34. Boller, *American Thought*, 118; see 117–19.

35. Russell H. Conwell, 'Acres of Diamonds', in Robert L. Ferm (ed.), *Issues in American Protestantism: A Documentary History from the Puritans to the Present*, Garden City: Doubleday, 1969, 235–42; quotations from 236–9.

36. Norman Vincent Peale, *The Power of Positive Thinking*, Lagos: Blessed Family Publishing, n.d., 22.

37. Ibid., 169.

38. Ibid., 77.

39. Cited in D. Hunt, *Beyond Seduction: A Return to Biblical Christianity*, Eugene, OR: Harvest House, 1987, 65.

40. Ibid., 66. Gloria Copeland insists, 'Tithing is absolutely the base. It is the only sure foundation for financial success' (*Voice of Victory*, 17/11, 12).

41. Douthat, *Bad Religion*, 194.

42. See whole discussion: Michael Schulson, 'Why Electing Donald Trump Was a Triumph for the Prosperity Gospel', *Washington Post*, 30 Nov.

2016, accessed 22 Nov. 2017. It is interesting to note that although the prosperity gospel has since made wide inroads into Britain, and indeed around the world, when John Patten, a Minister of State at the Home Office under Margaret Thatcher, called on the churches to develop a 'theology of success' (*Independent*, 14 Feb. 1989, 8), the Archbishop of Canterbury condemned the gospel of success as 'one of the worst heresies of the 20th century' (*Guardian*, 22 Feb. 1989, 3). *The Baptist Times* ran the headline 'Outrage at Call for "Success Theology"' (*Baptist Times*, 23 Feb. 1989, 20). See the discussion in *Tablet*, 4 March 1989, 264–5.

43. Churchwell, in plotting the evolution of the American dream, interestingly juxtaposes two books published in the boom year 1925. F. Scott Fitzgerald's *The Great Gatsby*, which initially sold only moderately, shows the narrowing of the American dream into materialism. Bruce Barton's *The Man Nobody Knows*, a bestseller of the next few years, made much of Jesus' statement that 'he must be about his father's business' (Luke 2.49) to argue that Jesus 'thought of his life as *business*' and was 'the founder of modern business'. Barton turned the New Testament into a business manual, and Churchwell concludes: 'A bestseller that calls Jesus the first great businessman is the *reductio ad absurdum* of America's long conflation of business with religion, its veneration of success, and its degraded Calvinist idea that personal wealth must mean God loves you more' (Sarah Churchwell, *Behold America: A History of America First and the American Dream*, London: Bloomsbury, 2018, 143).

44. Cited in Hanna Rosin, 'Did Christianity Cause the Crash?', *Atlantic*, Dec. 2009.

45. Kirbyjon Caldwell, *The Gospel of Good Success: A Road Map to Spiritual, Emotional, and Financial Wholeness*, New York: Simon and Schuster, 1999.

46. *Economist*, 20 May 2017, 40.

47. Cited in Rosin, 'Did Christianity'.

48. For a study of his rhetoric, see Helje Kringlebotn Sødal, '"Victor, not Victim": Joel Osteen's Rhetoric of Hope', *JCR*, 25, 1 (2010), 37–50.

49. Malcolm Gladwell, 'The Cellular Church: How Rick Warren's Congregation Grew', *The New Yorker*, 12 Sept. 2005, 64–5. Mark Twain called the Book of Mormon 'chloroform in print' (*Roughing It*, 1872, 58–9); *Purpose Driven Life* is a serious competitor for that distinction. Of course, Saddleback is big business as well. One Sunday in 2005 Warren called for a special offering 'Extend the Vision'; the offering was $7 million in cash and $53 million in commitments (Gladwell, 'Cellular Church', 63). Warren utilises these resources in considerable development outreach, not least in Africa. At the celebration in

Anaheim Angels' baseball stadium of the 25th anniversary of the church's founding, Rwanda's President Paul Kagame spoke to express his gratitude.

50. Paul Harris, 'How One Man's Self-Help Gospel Became a 20m Global Bestseller', *Observer*, 11 July 2004, 3.
51. Cited in Gladwell, 'Cellular Church', 63.
52. Alan Wolfe, 'Dieting for Jesus', *Prospect*, January 2004, 56.
53. Ibid., 55. Wolfe mentions churches offering a free appointment in a beauty parlour before joining. 'A religious movement that once preached abstinence and restraint now runs classes in the best way to reach orgasm' (ibid., 56).
54. Richard Reeves, 'Let's Get Motivated: A Hot Road Show Delivers a Gospel of Success. But Is It Religion or Commerce?', *Time*, 2 May 1994, 66–8. Reeves concludes: 'What bothered me was that so many people there wanted a new life, any new life. But that's what America has always been about, isn't it?'
55. Burtchaell, *Dying*, 561–2. Burtchaell admits his book is huge, and urges the reader to zoom in on what he or she knows best, and then move to the concluding chapter, but in fact his abundant data combined with opinionated asides make the entire 850 pages compulsive reading.
56. Ibid., 826.
57. Ibid., 830–1.
58. Ibid., 831.
59. Ibid., 849–50.
60. Ibid., 850; the ongoing debasement of rhetoric is a recurring theme: The self-presentation of the Lutheran Gettysburg College 'is so tenaciously enveloped in clouds of banality' (479); a 1981 Lutheran statement of partnership is characterised by 'uncommonly sonorous yet pointless assertions' (489). A Christian Reformed planning document 'appears as complex as the repair manual for a nuclear power plant' (805).
61. These influences are ably summarised, ibid., 837.
62. Ibid., 844.
63. Burtchaell is particularly hard on 'pietism', or the non-dogmatic and tradition-discounting forms of Christianity, professing 'the primacy of spirit over letter, commitment over institution, affect over intellect, laity over clergy, invisible church over visible, and [looking to] the earliest Christian communities for their models' (ibid., 839; see all 839–51).
64. Ibid., 563 & 851.
65. Ibid., 829.

66. Cardinal Newman Society website, accessed Jan. 2018.

67. Burtchaell, *Dying*, 822.

68. On this matter, see his treatment of the Jesuit Boston College, ibid., 578–82, 625–30. For many of these issues (treated rather poignantly), see Michael Hollerich, 'Do Catholic Theology Departments Have a Future?', *Commonweal*, 27 Mar. 2018, where sensing 'curricular Armageddon', he can write that 'our hold on the undergraduate curriculum … [is] disappearing faster than the Louisiana delta'.

69. Burtchaell, *Dying*, 850.

70. George M. Marsden, *The Outrageous Idea of Christian Scholarship*, New York: OUP, 1997, 1.

71. Ibid., 24.

72. Ibid., 10. Alan Wolfe deals with Wheaton, Fuller and Evangelical colleges in general and their rather paradoxical attempt to employ 'postmodernism' in their campaign to present their viewpoint as legitimate as any other, in 'The Opening of the Evangelical Mind', *Atlantic Monthly*, October 2000, 55–76.

73. Eagleton's discussion, based on the French philosopher Alain Badiou, of the way in which faith (in the sense of personal commitment) is involved in knowledge is perhaps the best part of his *Reason, Faith and Revolution* (116–22), but this is not Marsden's point.

74. Bob Priest's 'Missionary Positions: Christian, Modernist, Postmodernist', in *Current Anthropology*, 42 (2001), 29–68 argues similarly. One critic says the centre of gravity of the essay is: 'My subject position [as a believing Christian] gave me a perspective which helped me to see certain realities that were not as likely to be seen from another position but quite capable of being considered and evaluated once they were pointed out.' This 'may be true is some ways, but perhaps not in as deep a way as Priest asserts' (ibid., 57).

75. For these diverse strands, see Jay D. Green, *Christian Historiography: Five Rival Versions*, Waco: Baylor University Press, 2015.

76. Steinfels, *People Adrift*, 144.

77. Ibid., 151, italics in original. However, he confuses things somewhat by seeming to espouse Dennis O'Brien's position that religious truth 'has its own logic and demands its own method'; Catholic institutions 'would offer a different understanding of "the real", how one knows it and what that knowledge means for one's life' (ibid., 150). An equally sophisticated contribution about 'hiring for mission' does not go much further than Steinfels; John Garvey and Mark W. Roche, 'Hiring for Mission: Why It's Necessary, Why It's Hard', *Commonweal*, 10 Feb. 2017, 10–16.

78. Philip Gleason, *Contending with Modernity: Catholic Higher Education in the Twentieth Century*, New York: OUP, 1995, 320.

79. Steinfels, *People Adrift*, 204; also 141; see all 110–61, esp. 110–14. A simplistic use of labels renders Burtchaell's statistics problematic. He cites figures showing 'Catholic' students form the majority or second largest population at all sorts of 'Protestant' universities (Burtchaell, *Dying*, 835). If there is no significant difference between the denominational divisions of American youth, what is this supposed to indicate? 'Catholic' may indicate no more than 'of Catholic origin at a long-surpassed time when origins were important'.

80. Christian Smith, Kyle Longest, Jonathan Hill and Kari Christoffersen, *Young Catholic America: Emerging Adults in, out of, and Gone from the Church*, New York: OUP, 2014, 114. He concludes, 'American Catholicism as it is widely practiced and taught to youth, does not seem to have the cultural tools to counter [American consumerism]' (ibid., 229).

81. Melanie M. Morey and John J. Piderit, *Catholic Higher Education: A Culture in Crisis*, New York: OUP, 2006, fail to see that 'the Catholic intellectual tradition' was in large part devised in a world that has gone, so to promote it (which they understand as the role of a Catholic university) is far more problematic than they envisage.

82. A debate almost as fraught as those on the religion of Jefferson or Lincoln. For a characteristic treatment of Lincoln's Christianity, see Mencken, *Chrestomathy*, 221–3 [original edn 1922].

83. Barack Obama, *The Audacity of Hope: Thoughts on Reclaiming the American Dream*, New York: Three Rivers Press, 2006, 205–6.

84. According to Raban, 'His boss prepped him at his interview in New York: "If poor and working-class people want to build real power they have to have some sort of institutional base. With the unions in the shape they're in, the churches are the only game in town"', Jonathan Raban, 'Diary', *LRB*, 20 Mar. 2008, 47.

85. Christopher Hitchens reviewing David Remnick's *The Bridge: The Life and Rise of Barack Obama*, New York: Picador, 2010, in *Guardian*, 1 May 2010, 6. For Obama's religion, see also Lisa Miller and Richard Wolffe, 'Finding His Faith', *Newsweek*, 21 July 2008, 17–22.

86. Comically evident in the campaign of Howard Dean, at the time the front-runner for the 2004 Democratic presidential nomination, which was so secular he had to publicly do a U-turn, insisting he would henceforth 'include references to Jesus and God in my speeches as I stump in the South'. Revealingly, he insisted he had read the Bible from cover to cover, but named Job as his favourite book in the New Testament (*Tablet*, 10 Jan. 2004, 30; *Guardian*, 5 Jan. 2004, 15).

87. Simon Perfect, 'Barack Obama', in Spencer, *Mighty*, 252.

88. Christian Smith and Melina Lundquist Denton, *Soul Searching: The*

Religious and Spiritual Lives of American Teenagers, New York: OUP, 2005; Grace Davie in Berger et al., *Religious America*, 117.

89. Berger, *Adventures*, 132–3.
90. John Micklethwait and Adrian Wooldridge, *God Is Back: How the Global Revival of Faith Is Changing the World*, London: Penguin, 2009.

5. THE FUTURE

1. Riesebrodt, *Promise*, 12.
2. Cited in Ayer, *Part of My Life*, 131.
3. F. Halliday, *Nation and Religion in the Near East*, London: Saqi Books, 2000, 134, cited in Steve Bruce, *Politics and Religion*, Cambridge: Polity, 2003, 215.
4. J.D.Y. Peel, *Christianity, Islam and Orisa Religion: Three Traditions in Comparison and Interaction*, Oakland: University of California Press, 2016, 12.
5. Tony Judt, *The Memory Chalet*, London: Penguin, 2010, 209–10.
6. Discussed in Stefan Collini, 'Who Are the Spongers Now?', *LRB*, 21 Jan. 2016, 33.
7. Francis Fukuyama, *The End of History and the Last Man*, New York: Perennial, 2002 [1992], 335.
8. Gellner, *Plough*, 187 & 200; Ernest Gellner, *Postmodernism, Reason and Religion*, London: Routledge, 150; Grayling, *The Age of Genius*, 4–13; Wootton, *Invention*, 14; Fukuyama, *End of History*, 126–30; Weinberg, *To Explain the World*, 146; Mokyr, *Culture*, 250; Chadwick, *Secularization*, 144; Herbert Butterfield, *Man on his Past: The Study of the History of Historical Scholarship*, CUP, 1955, cited in Stefan Collini, *Common Reading: Critics, Historians, Publics*, OUP, 2008, 149.
9. Fukuyama, *Origins*, 460–2; Jeffrey Sachs, *The End of Poverty: How We Can Make It Happen in Our Lifetime*, London: Penguin, 2006, 26–50.
10. Johannes Fried (translated by Peter Lewis), *The Middle Ages*, Cambridge, MA: Harvard University Press, 2015, 81. Also: 'The effects and ramifications of these medieval waves of learning and research, observation, reflection, and experimentation are still very tangibly present nowadays. The general principle of scholarship, the Western culture of rationality, the Enlightenment, and globalization can all trace their origins back to this period' (ibid., 516–17).
11. Mokyr, *Culture*, 338.
12. Grayling, *Age of Genius*, 315.
13. Stephen Jay Gould, *Rocks of Ages: Science and Religion in the Fullness of Life*, New York: Ballantine Books, 2002.
14. Richard Dawkins, *The God Delusion*, London: Bantam, 2006, 54–61

(where he also argues that science is no less qualified to address ultimate questions than religion).

15. Grayling, *Age of Genius*, 315.
16. Ibid., 321.
17. David S. Landes, *The Unbound Prometheus*, CUP, 1969, 6; Landes wrote 'twentieth century'.
18. For a list of 48 characteristics of modernity, see Norman Davies, *Europe: A History*, OUP, 1996, 1293. Beckford is concerned to stress the changes from Industrial to Advanced Industrial Society, but interestingly he lists them as predominantly *moral* issues: nuclear threat; intensification of civil and military conflicts; moral dilemmas of globalisation and ecology; worsening plight of the third world; deskilling of workforce; family breakdown; growth of single issue politics; concentration of media power and so on (*Religion and Advanced*, 169). I have been less concerned with the problems they bring than acknowledging their reality.
19. Berger, *Adventures*, 234–5. It is unclear here whether for Berger the multiplicity applies to modernity itself, or the *paths to* modernity.
20. Ibid., 147.
21. Ibid., 238–9.
22. Words attributed to Philip Jenkins in Toby Lester, 'Oh, Gods!', *Atlantic Monthly*, Feb. 2002. Eagleton again misses the point in writing that 'a supercivilized brand of cultural supremacism, one which would no doubt find itself offended by common-or-garden racism, is now much in fashion', *Reason, Faith and Revolution*, 95.
23. Gellner, *Postmodernism*, 61.
24. Ernest Gellner, 'Anything Goes', *TLS*, 16 June 1995, 8.
25. Gellner, *Postmodernism*, 82.
26. Ibid., 61.
27. Gellner describes functional rationality as 'the cold, calculating, single-minded choice of means for a given end' (*Plough*, 128). Activity is subjected 'to the criteria of effectiveness alone' (ibid., 276). When each activity is endowed with 'a single aim, a single criterion, it makes it possible to judge, assess and hence improve efficiency' (ibid., 208), so means-ends or single-end rationality or instrumental efficiency through the use of objective criteria triumphs. Beckford's claim that 'There is no necessary incompatibility between religion and rationality. In theory, at least, rational inquiry, empirically confirmed scientific knowledge and the pursuit of efficiency can all be accommodated within a world-view based on religious faith' (*Social Theory*, 48) is hard to assess, for of set purpose he gives us no idea of what he means by 'religious faith'.

28. Well covered in the nation's media. See *Independent*, 5 June 2003, 1; *Guide*, 24 June 2003, 8; *Independent*, 26 June 2003, 3; *Chronicle*, 26 June 2003, 2; *Chronicle*, 15 July 2003, 1; and BBC News, 16 June 2003.

29. Samuel Huntington, *Political Order in Changing Societies*, New Haven: Yale University Press, 2006; Fukuyama, *Origins*, 458–60.

30. 'Earthly Concerns', *Economist*, 18 Aug. 2012, 17–18.

31. Alexander Stille, 'Holy Orders', *New Yorker*, 14 Sept. 2015.

32. *Tablet*, 27 May 2017, 29.

33. Spencer, *Future*, 44–6.

34. Grace Davie, 'Vicarious Religion: A Response', *JCR*, 25 (2010), 266.

35. Somewhat like Britain's monarchy; see Bill McSweeney, *Roman Catholicism: The Search for Relevance*, Oxford: Blackwell, 1980, 231.

36. John L. Allen, *The Future Church: How Ten Trends Are Revolutionizing the Catholic Church*, New York: Doubleday, 2009.

37. Ibid., 410; see also 434–5.

38. For the NGO-isation of Christianity, see Gifford, *Christianity, Development and Modernity*, especially my discussion (79–80) of José Casanova, 'Global Catholicism and the Politics of Civil Society', *Sociological Inquiry*, 66, 3 (1996), 356–73.

39. Newman, *Apologia*, 227; in this case, the doctrine of the Immaculate Conception of Mary.

40. Ibid., 265–71.

41. Anthony Kenny, *A Path from Rome*, OUP, 1986, 78. Bruce's detection of 'a major difference between, at the two extremes, the democratic epistemology of radical Protestantism and the exclusive epistemology of the Catholic Church' (*God Is Dead*, 157) is anachronistic.

42. Woodward, *Getting Religion*, 235–6, citing John Paul II in 1994.

43. Australian Associated Press, 18 Oct. 2014.

44. John Henry Newman, *The Idea of a University*, New Haven: Yale University Press, 1996 [1852], 19.

45. Ibid., 154.

46. Newman, *Apologia*, 344–5; see all 252–62.

47. Steve Bruce, 'Religion in Britain at the Close of the 20th Century: A Challenge to the Silver Lining Perspective', *JCR*, 11 (1996), 272. The two studies mentioned here are L. Davidoff and C. Hall, *Family Fortunes: Men and Women of the English Middle Class 1780–1850*, London: Routledge, 1992, and P. Abrams and R. Brown (eds.), *UK Society*, London: Weidenfeld and Nicolson, 1984. To take a study of a significant British social institution almost at random, Vinen's study of Britain's national service hardly mentions religion, except to comment that loss of faith 'seems to have happened [to national servicemen]

even faster than it did to ordinary young men in the 1950s', and 'even
the most optimistic military authorities recognized that religion had
little impact on the morality of servicemen' (Richard Vinen, *National
Service: A Generation in Uniform*, London: Penguin, 2015 [2014], 172 &
180).

48. Noel Annan, *Our Age: Portrait of a Generation*, London: Weidenfeld and
Nicolson, 1990, 38.

49. Ibid., 299–300. Immediately before this, he notes the 'transformation
of the Christian message' in the 1960s, in accordance with my argument here. 'The liver and lungs were torn out of the old theology
leaving the heart still beating.' It was 'selfish and otiose to concern
ourselves with our own personal salvation. We should therefore concern ourselves with the poor at home and plight of the Third World
abroad ... All the churches, Rome as well as the Protestant communities, heard this call and Our Age witnessed the reorientation of
Christian faith.'

50. James Stourton, *Kenneth Clark: Life, Art and Civilization*, London: Collins,
2016, 343. Clark enigmatically does refer to a 'religious experience'
in his earlier life (Kenneth Clark, *The Other Half*, London: John
Murray, 1977, 108), and for a 'reported conversion' on his deathbed,
see Stourton, *Kenneth Clark*, 399.

51. Carey, *The Unexpected Professor*, 123. Introducing the otherworldly
dimension seems to cause almost insuperable difficulties in high art,
as Colm Tóibín suggests in reviewing the novelist Marilynne Robinson,
who is almost unique today not only in writing about religious figures
in religious settings, but in bringing a religious perspective to them—
she writes as a confessed Calvinist, seeing undeserved grace underlying everything. Tóibín remarks: 'God represents a real problem for the
novelist ... How do you create a religious or a non-secular protago-
nist in a novel without making a dog's dinner out of the book?' (Colm
Tóibín, 'Putting Religion in Its Place', *LRB*, 23 Oct. 2014).

52. Brown, *The Death of Christian Britain*, 181–90. Brown admits this discursive change is not evident in the United States where the culture
wars have kept traditional rhetoric before the public in a way not seen
in Europe (ibid., 197).

53. Peter L. Berger, 'Introduction: The Cultural Dynamics of Globalization',
in Peter L. Berger and Samuel P. Huntington, *Many Globalizations:
Cultural Diversity in the Contemporary World*, New York: OUP, 2002, 3–6.

54. J.M. Roberts, *The Triumph of the West*, London: Little, Brown, 1985,
37.

55. Robert Butterworth, *The Detour: Towards Revising Catholicism*, Leominster:
Gracewing, 2005, 101. So too Kenny: 'Even from the point of view

of a secular historian of ideas, the Christian and Catholic system, if not a revelation from God, is one of the most fascinating inventions of the human spirit; a construction erected by the best minds of many generations' (Kenny, *Path*, 77–8).

56. Philip Jenkins, *The Next Christendom: The Coming of Global Christianity*, New York: OUP, 2002, 198 & 202.

57. Christopher Comoro and John Sivalon, 'Marian Faith Healing Ministry', in Thomas Bamat and F. Wiest (eds.), *Popular Catholicism in a World Church: Seven Case Studies in Inculturation*, Maryknoll, NY: Orbis, 1998, 170.

58. John Gray, 'The Myth of Secularism', *New Statesman*, 16–30 Dec. 2002, 70.

59. R.N. Bellah, *Beyond Belief*, New York: Harper and Row, 1970, 223.

60. Jonathan Sacks, 'The Meaning-Seeking Animal', 2009 annual Theos lecture, www.theosthinktank.co.uk; accessed 12 Dec. 2017.

61. Felipe Fernández-Armesto, *The Future of Religion*, London: Phoenix, 1997, 52.

62. Ibid., 53.

63. Ibid.

64. Berger, *Rumour*, 30.

65. Pippa Norris and Ronald Inglehart, *Sacred and Secular: Religion and Politics Worldwide*, 2nd edn, CUP, 2011. Bruce provides a stimulating reworking of their theory in terms of plausibility rather than prosperity and peace (*Secularization*, 194–9).

66. William James, *Varieties of Religious Experience*, London: Penguin, 1982 [1902], 162.

67. Martin Riesebrodt, 'Religion in Global Perspective', in Mark Juergensmeyer (ed.), *Global Religions: An Introduction*, New York: OUP, 2003, 95–109 (see all 107–8). Riesebrodt exemplifies the confusion characteristic of so many scholars of religion. Having defined religion substantively, he can talk of 'the resurgence of religion' referring to sections in bookshops devoted to 'spirituality, esotericism, or self-help' (*Promise*, 178). That this spirituality, esotericism and self-help have any relation to a supernatural realm and thus meet the requirements of his substantive definition cannot simply be presumed.

68. Max Weber, *Science as a Vocation* [1918], cited in Wootton, *Invention*, 449.

69. Andrew Brown and Linda Woodhead, *That Was the Church That Was: How the Church of England Lost the English People*, London: Bloomsbury, 2016, 190–3.

70. Kevin N. Flatt, *After Evangelicalism: The Sixties and the United Church of Canada*, Montreal and Kingston: MQUP, 2013, 239.

71. Ibid., 241.

72. Smith, *American Evangelicalism: Embattled and Thriving*.

73. Flatt, *After Evangelicalism*, 230–1.

74. Ibid., 244.

75. Steinfels, *People Adrift*, 229.

76. Smith et al., *Young Catholic America*, 14. This floundering brought 'harmful ambiguity, hesitation and misdirection'.

77. Alister McGrath, *The Future of Christianity*, Oxford: Blackwell, 2002, 101 & 121–8.

78. Ibid., 25 & 137.

79. Ibid., 19, 123.

80. Dawkins, *The God Delusion*; Harris, *Letter to a Christian Nation*; Christopher Hitchens, *God Is Not Great: How Religion Poisons Everything*, New York: Twelve, 2007.

81. Don Cupitt, *Taking Leave of God*, London: SCM, 1980; and *After God: The Future of Religion*, London: Basic Books, 1999. Lloyd Geering, *Tomorrow's God*, Wellington: Bridget Williams, 1994, and Lloyd Geering, *The World to Come: From Christian Past to Global Future*, Wellington: Bridget Williams, 1999. Whether the less ambitious approach adopted by the likes of Martin Prozesky has legs remains to be seen. His *Conscience: Ethical Intelligence for Global Well-Being*, Scottsville: University of KwaZulu-Natal Press, 2007, though respectful towards religions of the past (he's writing in South Africa) is an unashamed guide to 'post-religious living'. 'Atheist vicars' seem like people thinking their way out of traditional Christianity rather than a hope for the future (Kirsty Milne, 'God in the Dock', *New Statesman and Society*, 1 April 1994, 16–18). The phenomenon of less rigid forms enabling an individual to escape a straitjacket while furthering overall decline is well treated in Bruce, *God Is Dead*, 184–5.

82. Eagleton, *Reason, Faith and Revolution*, 70.

83. Bossy, *Christianity*, vii–viii & 97.

84. Bruce, *Choice*, 185–6.

85. Berger, *Questions*, 45.

SELECT BIBLIOGRAPHY

Aaronovitch, David, *Party Animals: My Family and Other Communists*, London: Vintage, 2017 [2016].

Allen, John L., *The Future Church: How Ten Trends Are Revolutionizing the Catholic Church*, New York: Doubleday, 2009.

Annan, Noel, *Our Age: Portrait of a Generation*, London: Weidenfeld and Nicolson, 1990.

Atkin, Nicholas and Frank Tallett, *Priests, Prelates and People: A History of European Catholicism since 1750*, New York: OUP, 2003.

Ayer, A.J., *Part of My Life*, London: Collins, 1977.

Bamat, Thomas and F. Wiest (eds), *Popular Catholicism in a World Church: Seven Case Studies in Inculturation*, Maryknoll, NY: Orbis, 1998.

Barnes, Philip L., 'Was the Northern Ireland Conflict Religious?', *JCR*, 20 (2005), 55–69.

Beckford, James A., *Religion and Advanced Industrial Society*, London: Routledge, 1989.

————, *Social Theory and Religion*, Cambridge: CUP, 2003.

Bellah, R.N., *Beyond Belief*, New York: Harper and Row, 1970.

Berger, Peter L., *A Rumour of Angels: Modern Society and the Rediscovery of the Supernatural*, London: Penguin, 1970 [1969].

————, Brigitte Berger and Hansfried Kellner, *The Homeless Mind: Modernization and Consciousness*, London: Penguin, 1974.

————, *The Sacred Canopy: Elements of a Sociological Theory of Religion*, New York: Anchor Books, 1990 [1969].

————, *Questions of Faith: A Skeptical Affirmation of Christianity*, Oxford: Blackwell, 2004.

————, and Samuel P. Huntington, *Many Globalizations: Cultural Diversity in the Contemporary World*, New York: OUP, 2002.

————, Grace Davie and Effie Fokas, *Religious America, Secular Europe? A Theme and Variations*, Aldershot: Ashgate, 2008.

SELECT BIBLIOGRAPHY

————, *Adventures of an Accidental Sociologist: How to Explain the World without Becoming a Bore*, Amherst: Prometheus Books, 2011.

Bloom, Harold, *The American Religion: The Emergence of the Post-Christian Nation*, New York: Simon and Schuster, 1992.

Boller, Paul F., *American Thought in Transition: The Impact of Evolutionary Naturalism 1865–1900*, Chicago: Rand McNally, 1969.

Bossy, John, *Christianity in the West 1400–1700*, Oxford: OUP, 1985.

Brenan, Gerald, *The Spanish Labyrinth*, 2nd edn, Cambridge: CUP, 2014 [1950].

Brown, Andrew and Linda Woodhead, *That Was the Church That Was: How the Church of England Lost the English People*, London: Bloomsbury, 2016.

Brown, Callum G., *The Death of Christian Britain*, London: Routledge, 2001.

————, *Religion and Society in Twentieth Century Britain*, Harlow: Pearson, 2006.

Bruce, Steve, 'Religion in Britain at the Close of the 20th Century: A Challenge to the Silver Lining Perspective', *JCR*, 11 (1996), 261–75.

————, 'The Pervasive World View: Religion in Pre-Modern Britain', *British Journal of Sociology*, 48, 4 (1997), 667–80.

————, *Choice and Religion: A Critique of Rational Choice*, Oxford: OUP, 1999.

————, *Secularization: In Defence of an Unfashionable Theory*, Oxford: OUP, 2001.

————, *God Is Dead: Secularization in the West*, Oxford: Blackwell, 2002.

————, 'Praying Alone? Church-going in Britain and the Putnam Thesis', *JCR*, 17, 3 (2002), 317–28.

————, *Politics and Religion*, Cambridge: Polity, 2003.

————, 'Secularization: The Impotence of Individualized Religion', *The Hedgehog Review: After Secularization*, 8 (2006), 35–45.

————, *Paisley: Religion and Politics in Northern Ireland*, New York: OUP, 2007.

————, 'Religion in the Northern Ireland Conflict', *Annali di storia dell'esegesi*, 26, 2 (2009), 301–23.

————, 'Defining Religion: A Practical Response', *International Review of Sociology*, 21, 1 (2011), 107–20.

————, 'Post-Secularity and Religion in Britain: An Empirical Assessment', *JCR*, 28 (2013), 369–84.

————, and Tony Glendenning, 'When Was Secularization? Dating the Decline of the British Churches and Locating Its Cause', *British Journal of Sociology*, 61, 1 (2010), 107–26.

————, and David Voas, 'Vicarious Religion: An Examination and Critique', *JCR*, 25, 2 (2010), 243–59.

Burtchaell, James Tunstead, *The Dying of the Light: The Disengagement of Colleges and Universities from Their Christian Churches*, Grand Rapids: Eerdmans, 1998.

Butterworth, Robert, *The Detour: Towards Revising Catholicism*, Leominster: Gracewing, 2005.

SELECT BIBLIOGRAPHY

Caldwell, Kirbyjon, *The Gospel of Good Success: A Road Map to Spiritual, Emotional, and Financial Wholeness*, New York: Simon and Schuster, 1999.

Cameron, Euan, *Enchanted Europe: Superstition, Reason, and Religion 1250–1750*, New York: OUP, 2010.

Carey, John, *The Unexpected Professor: An Oxford Life in Books*, London: Faber and Faber, 2014.

Carpenter, Joel A., *Revive Us Again: The Reawakening of American Fundamentalism*, New York: OUP, 1997.

Casanova, José, 'Global Catholicism and the Politics of Civil Society', *Sociological Inquiry*, 66, 3 (1996), 356–73.

———, 'Rethinking Secularization: A Global Comparative Perspective', *The Hedgehog Review: After Secularization*, 8 (2006), 7–22.

Cavanaugh, William, *The Myth of Religious Violence*, New York: OUP, 2009.

Chadwick, Owen, *The Secularization of the European Mind in the Nineteenth Century*, Oxford: OUP, 1975.

Chadwick, Owen, *The Popes and European Revolution*, Oxford: OUP, 1981.

———, *A History of the Popes 1830–1914*, Oxford: OUP, 1998.

Churchwell, Sarah, *Behold America: A History of America First and the American Dream*, London: Bloomsbury, 2018.

Clark, Kenneth, *The Other Half*, London: John Murray, 1977.

Collingwood, R.G., *An Autobiography*, Oxford: OUP, with new intro. by Stephen Toulmin, 1978 [1939].

Collini, Stefan, *Matthew Arnold: A Critical Portrait*, Oxford: OUP, 1994.

———, *Common Reading: Critics, Historians, Publics*, Oxford: OUP, 2008.

———, 'What's Not to Like?', *LRB*, 2 June 2011, 10–12 (a review of John A. Hall, *Ernest Gellner: An Intellectual Biography*, London: Verso, 2010).

———, 'Who Are the Spongers Now?', *LRB*, 21 January 2016, 33–7.

Commager, H.S., *The American Mind: An Interpretation of American Thought and Character since the 1880s*, New Haven: Yale University Press, 1950.

Connolly, William E., *Capitalism and Christianity, American Style*, Durham: Duke University Press, 2008.

Crockett, Alasdair and David Voas, 'Generations of Decline: Religious Change in Twentieth Century Britain', *Journal for the Scientific Study of Religion*, 45, 4 (2006), 567–84.

Cupitt, Don, *Taking Leave of God*, London: SCM, 1980.

———, *After God: The Future of Religion*, London: Basic Books, 1999.

———, *The Meaning of the West: An Apologia for Secular Christianity*, London: SCM, 2008.

Davenport-Hines, Richard (ed.), *Letters from Oxford: Hugh Trevor-Roper to Bernard Berenson*, London: Phoenix, 2006.

———, *Religion in Britain since 1945: Believing without Belonging*, Oxford: Blackwell, 1994.

SELECT BIBLIOGRAPHY

————, *Religion in Modern Europe: A Memory Mutates*, Oxford: OUP, 2000.

Davie, Grace, 'A Reply to Steve Bruce', *JCR*, 17, 3 (2002), 329–34.

————, 'Vicarious Religion: A Response', *JCR*, 25, 2 (2010), 261–6.

Davies, Norman, *Europe: A History*, Oxford: OUP, 1996.

Dawkins, Richard, *A Devil's Chaplain*, London: Weidenfeld and Nicolson, 2003.

————, *The God Delusion*, London: Bantam, 2006.

Day, Dorothy, *The Long Loneliness*, New York: HarperCollins, 1997 [1952].

Douthat, Ross, *Bad Religion: How We Became a Nation of Heretics*, New York: Free Press, 2012.

Dummett, Michael, 'A Remarkable Consensus', *New Blackfriars*, 68 (1987), 424–31.

————, Unsafe Premises: A Reply to Nicholas Lash', *New Blackfriars*, 68 (1987), 558–66.

Dworkin, Ronald, 'Religion without God', *NYRB*, 4 April 2013, 67–74.

Eagleton, Terry, *The Meaning of Life: A Very Short Introduction*, Oxford: OUP, 2007.

————, *Reason, Faith and Revolution: Reflections on the God Debate*, New Haven and London: Yale University Press, 2009.

————, *Culture and the Death of God*, New Haven and London: Yale University Press, 2015.

Erdozain, Dominic, *Soul of Doubt: The Religious Roots of Unbelief from Luther to Marx*, New York: OUP, 2016.

Fernández-Armesto, Felipe, *The Future of Religion*, London: Phoenix, 1997.

Fitzgerald, Frances, *The Evangelicals: The Struggle to Shape America*, New York: Simon and Schuster, 2017.

Flatt, Kevin N., *After Evangelicalism: The Sixties and the United Church of Canada*, Montreal and Kingston: MQUP, 2013.

Fried, Johannes (translated by Peter Lewis), *The Middle Ages*, Cambridge, MA: Harvard University Press, 2015.

Fukuyama, Francis, *The End of History and the Last Man*, New York: Perennial, 2002 [1992].

————, *The Origins of Political Order: From Prehuman Times to the French Revolution*, New York: Farrar, Straus and Giroux, 2011.

Fulton, John, *The Tragedy of Belief: Division, Politics, and Religion in Ireland*, Oxford: OUP, 1991.

————, 'Sociology, Religion and "The Troubles" in Northern Ireland: A Critical Approach', *Economic and Social Review*, 20 (1988), 5–24.

————, 'Religion and Enmity in Ireland: Institutions and Relational Beliefs', *Social Compass*, 49 (2002), 189–202.

Galbraith, John Kenneth, *The Age of Uncertainty*, London: BBC/André Deutsch, 1977.

Garvey, John and Mark W. Roche, 'Hiring for Mission: Why It's Necessary, Why It's Hard', *Commonweal*, 10 February 2017, 10–16.

Geering, Lloyd, *Tomorrow's God*, Wellington: Bridget Williams, 1994.

————, *The World to Come: From Christian Past to Global Future*, Wellington: Bridget Williams, 1999.

Gellner, Ernest, *Postmodernism, Reason and Religion*, London: Routledge, 1992.

————, 'Anything Goes', *TLS*, 16 June 1995, 6–8.

————, 'The Importance of Being Modular', in John A. Hall (ed.), *Civil Society: Theory, History, Comparison*, Cambridge: Polity Press, 1995, 32–55.

————, *Plough, Sword and Book: The Structure of Human History*, London: Collins Harvill, 1988.

Giddens, Anthony, *Sociology*, Cambridge: Polity Press, 2006.

Gifford, Paul, *Christianity and Politics in Doe's Liberia*, Cambridge: CUP, 1993.

————, 'A Contemporary Nigerian Reading of the Bible', *Journal of Theology for Southern Africa*, 152 (2015), 38–56.

————, *Christianity, Development and Modernity in Africa*, London: Hurst, 2015.

————, 'A Nigerian Reading of the Bible and Its Interpretational Power', in Klaus Hock (ed.), *The Power of Interpretation: Imagined Authenticity, Appropriated Identity: Conflicting Discourses on New Forms of African Christianity*, Wiesbaden: Harrassowitz Verlag, 2016, 25–37.

————, 'Religion in Contemporary Senegal', *JCR*, 31, 2 (2016), 255–67.

Gladwell, Malcolm, 'The Cellular Church: How Rick Warren's Congregation Grew', *The New Yorker*, 12 September 2005, 60–7.

Gleason, Philip, *Contending with Modernity: Catholic Higher Education in the Twentieth Century*, New York: OUP, 1995.

Goodall, Norman (ed.), *The Uppsala Report 1968: Official Report of the Fourth Assembly of the World Council of Churches, Uppsala, July 4–20 1968*, Geneva: WCC, 1968.

Gould, Stephen Jay, *Rocks of Ages: Science and Religion in the Fullness of Life*, New York: Ballantine Books, 2002.

Grayling, A.C., *The Age of Genius: The Seventeenth Century and the Birth of the Modern Mind*, London: Bloomsbury, 2015.

Green, Jay D., *Christian Historiography: Five Rival Versions*, Waco: Baylor University Press, 2015.

Gregory, Brad S., *The Unintended Reformation: How a Religious Reformation Secularized Society*, Cambridge, MA: Belknap/Harvard, 2012.

Gribbin, John, *Science: A History*, London: Penguin, 2003 [2002].

Hadaway, C. Kirk, Penny Long Marler and Mark Chaves, 'What the Polls Don't Show: A Closer Look at US Church Attendance', *American Sociological Review*, 58 (1993), 741–52.

Hare, David, *Asking Around*, London: Faber and Faber, 1993.

SELECT BIBLIOGRAPHY

Harris, Sam, *Letter to a Christian Nation: A Challenge to Faith*, London: Bantam Press, 2007 [2006].

Harvey, Van A., 'Is There an Ethics of Belief?' *Journal of Religion*, 49, 1 (1969), 41–58.

———, 'The Ethics of Belief Reconsidered', *Journal of Religion*, 59, 4 (1979), 406–20.

Hayden, J. Michael, *The Catholicisms of Coutances: Varieties of Religion in Early Modern France 1350–1789*, Montreal and Kingston, MQUP, 2013.

Herberg, Will, *Protestant-Catholic-Jew*, New York: Doubleday, 1960 [1955].

Hervieu-Léger, Danièle, *Religion as a Chain of Memory*, Cambridge: Polity, 2000 [1993].

Himmelfarb, Gertrude, *The Roads to Modernity: The British, French and American Enlightenments*, London: Vintage, 2008 [2004].

Hitchens, Christopher, *God Is Not Great: How Religion Poisons Everything*, New York: Twelve, 2007.

Hobson, Theo, *God Created Humanism: The Christian Basis of Secular Values*, London: SPCK, 2017.

Hofstadter, Richard, *Social Darwinism in American Thought 1850–1915*, Philadelphia: University of Pennsylvania Press, 1945.

Hoge, Dean R., 'Core and Periphery in American Catholic Teaching', *JCR*, 17 (2002), 293–302.

Hoggart, Richard, *Uses of Literacy*, London: Penguin, 2009 [1957].

Hollerich, Michael, 'Do Catholic Theology Departments Have a Future?', *Commonweal*, 27 March 2018, Commonweal website.

Horton, Robin, 'African Conversion', *Africa*, 41 (1971), 85–108.

Houlden, J.L., *Bible and Belief*, London: SPCK, 1991.

Howard, Thomas Albert, *God and the Atlantic: America, Europe and the Religious Divide*, New York: OUP, 2011.

Hunt, D., *Beyond Seduction: A Return to Biblical Christianity*, Eugene, OR: Harvest House, 1987.

Huntington, Samuel, *Political Order in Changing Societies*, New Haven: Yale University Press, 2006.

Hurd, Elizabeth Shakman, *Beyond Religious Freedom: The New Global Politics of Religion*, Princeton: Princeton University Press, 2016.

Ingliss, Tom, 'Catholic Identity in Contemporary Ireland: Belief and Belonging to Tradition', *JCR*, 22 (2007), 205–20.

James, William, *Varieties of Religious Experience*, London: Penguin, 1982 [1902].

Jenkins, Philip, *The Next Christendom: The Coming of Global Christianity*, New York: OUP, 2002.

———, 'Christianity Moves South', in Frans Wijsen and Robert Schreiter (eds.), *Global Christianity: Contested Claims*, Amsterdam and New York: Rodophi, 2007.

SELECT BIBLIOGRAPHY

Judt, Tony, *The Memory Chalet*, London: Penguin, 2010.

Kenny, Anthony, *A Path from Rome*, Oxford: OUP, 1986.

Kessler, Gary E., *Fifty Key Thinkers on Religion*, Abingdon: Routledge, 2012.

Küng, Hans, *Christianity: The Religious Situation of our Time*, London: SCM, 1995 [German edn, 1994].

―――, *Eternal Life?*, London: HarperCollins, 1984.

Ladurie, Emmanuel Le Roy, *Mountaillou: Cathars and Catholics in a French Village 1294–1324*, London: Penguin, 1980 [1978].

Landes, David S., *The Unbound Prometheus*, Cambridge: CUP, 1969.

―――, *The Wealth and Poverty of Nations: Why Some Are So Rich and Some So Poor*, London: Little, Brown, 1998.

Lash, Nicholas, 'A Leaky Sort of Thing? The Divisiveness of Michael Dummett', *New Blackfriars*, 68 (1987), 552–7.

Lewis, Bernard (and Buntzie Ellis Churchill), *Notes on a Century: Reflections of a Middle East Historian*, London: Weidenfeld and Nicolson, 2012.

Lienhardt, G., *Divinity and Experience: The Religion of the Dinka*, Oxford: OUP, 1961.

Linker, Damon, *The Theocons: Secular America under Siege*, New York: Anchor Books, 2006.

Lodge, David, *How Far Can You Go?*, London: Penguin, 1981 [1980].

―――, *The British Museum Is Falling Down*, London: Penguin, 1983 [1965].

―――, *Paradise News*, London: Penguin, 1992.

MacCulloch, Diarmaid, 'Tidy-mindedness', *LRB*, 37, 18 (24 September 2015), 17–18.

Madigan, Timothy J., *W.K. Clifford and 'The Ethics of Belief'*, Newcastle: Cambridge Scholars Publishing, 2009.

Marsden, George M., *Fundamentalism and American Culture: The Shaping of Twentieth-Century Evangelicalism 1870–1925*, New York: OUP, 1980.

―――, *The Outrageous Idea of Christian Scholarship*, New York: OUP, 1997.

Martin, David, *A General Theory of Secularization*, Oxford: Blackwell, 1978.

―――, *Does Religion Cause War?*, Oxford: OUP, 2004.

―――, *The Education of David Martin*, London: SPCK, 2013.

McGrath, Alister, *The Future of Christianity*, Oxford: Blackwell, 2002.

McKibbin, Ross, *Classes and Cultures: England 1918–1951*, New York: OUP, 1998.

McLeod, Hugh, *Religion and the People of Western Europe 1789–1989*, new edn, Oxford: OUP, 1997.

―――, *The Religious Crisis of the 1960s*, Oxford: OUP, 2007.

McSweeney, Bill, *Roman Catholicism: The Search for Relevance*, Oxford: Blackwell, 1980.

Merton, Robert K., 'Science, Technology and Society in Seventeenth-Century England', *Osiris*, 4 (1938), 360–632.

Micklethwait, John and Adrian Wooldridge, *God Is Back: How the Global Revival of Faith Is Changing the World*, London: Penguin, 2009.

Mill, John Stuart, *The Autobiography*, npl: ReadaClassic, 2010 [1873].

Mokyr, Joel, *A Culture of Growth: The Origins of the Modern Economy*, Princeton: Princeton University Press, 2017.

Morey, Melanie M. and John J. Piderit, *Catholic Higher Education: A Culture in Crisis*, New York: OUP, 2006.

Newman, John Henry, *Apologia pro Vita Sua*, London: Penguin, 1994 [1864].

————, *The Idea of a University*, New Haven: Yale University Press, 1996 [1852].

Nineham, Dennis, *Christianity Mediaeval and Modern*, London: SCM, 1993.

Norris, Pippa and Ronald Inglehart, *Sacred and Secular: Religion and Politics Worldwide*, 2nd edn, Cambridge: CUP, 2011.

Nye, Malory, *Religion: The Basics*, London: Routledge, 2003.

Obama, Barack, *The Audacity of Hope: Thoughts on Reclaiming the American Dream*, New York: Three Rivers Press, 2006.

Oldridge, Darren, *The Supernatural in Tudor and Stuart England*, London: Routledge, 2016.

O'Malley, John W., *What Happened at Vatican II?*, Cambridge, MA: Harvard University Press, 2008.

————, *Trent: What Happened at the Council*, Cambridge, MA: Belknap/Harvard, 2013.

Peale, Norman Vincent, *The Power of Positive Thinking*, Lagos: Blessed Family Publishing, n.d..

Peel, J.D.Y., *Religious Encounter and the Making of the Yoruba*, Bloomington and Indianapolis: Indiana University Press, 2000.

————, *Christianity, Islam and Orisa Religion: Three Traditions in Comparison and Interaction*, Oakland: University of California Press, 2016.

Priest, Bob, 'Missionary Positions: Christian, Modernist, Postmodernist', *Current Anthropology*, 42 (2001), 29–68.

Prozesky, Martin, *Conscience: Ethical Intelligence for Global Well-Being*, Scottsville: University of KwaZulu-Natal Press, 2007.

Putnam, Robert D., *Bowling Alone: The Collapse and Revival of American Community*, New York: Simon and Schuster, 2000.

Reeves, Richard, 'Let's Get Motivated: A Hot Road Show Delivers a Gospel of Success. But Is It Religion or Commerce?', *Time*, 2 May 1994, 66–8.

Riesebrodt, Martin, 'Religion in Global Perspective', in Mark Juergensmeyer (ed.), *Global Religions: An Introduction*, New York: OUP, 2003, 95–109.

————, *The Promise of Salvation: A Theory of Religion*, Chicago and London: University of Chicago Press, 2010.

Roberts, J.M., *The Triumph of the West*, London: Little, Brown, 1985.

Roper, Lyndal, *Martin Luther: Renegade and Prophet*, London: Vintage, 2017 [2016].

SELECT BIBLIOGRAPHY

Rosen, William, *Justinian's Flea: Plague, Empire and the Birth of Europe*, London: Pimlico, 2008 [2006].

Rosin, Hanna, 'Did Christianity Cause the Crash?', *Atlantic*, December 2009.

Rufin, Jean-Christophe, *Immortelle randonnée. Compostelle malgré moi*, Paris: Gallimard, 2013.

Sachs, Jeffrey, *The End of Poverty: How We Can Make It Happen in Our Lifetime*, London: Penguin, 2006.

Shapin, Steven, *The Scientific Revolution*, Chicago: University of Chicago Press, 1996.

Sheed, Wilfred, *Essays in Disguise*, New York: Alfred A. Knopf, 1990.

Sheehan, Thomas, 'Revolution in the Church', *NYRB*, 14 June 1984, 35–9.

Siedentop, Larry, *Inventing the Individual: The Origins of Western Liberalism*, London: Penguin 2015 [2014].

Sisman, Adam, *Hugh Trevor-Roper: The Biography*, London: Weidenfeld and Nicolson, 2010.

Smith, Christian, *American Evangelicalism: Embattled and Thriving*, Chicago: University of Chicago Press, 1998.

Smith, Christian and Melina Lundquist Denton, *Soul Searching: The Religious and Spiritual Lives of American Teenagers*, New York: OUP, 2005.

Smith, Christian, Kyle Longest, Jonathan Hill and Kari Christoffersen, *Young Catholic America: Emerging Adults in, out of, and Gone from the Church*, New York: OUP, 2014.

Smith, Wilfred Cantwell, *What Is Scripture?*, London: SCM, 1989.

Smith, Zadie, 'On Optimism and Despair', address given in Berlin, 10 November 2016 on receiving Welt Literature Prize, in *NYRB*, 22 December 2016.

Sødal, Helje Kringlebotn, '"Victor, Not Victim": Joel Osteen's Rhetoric of Hope', *JCR*, 25, 1 (2010), 37–50.

Sow, Ibrahima, *Divination, marabout, destin. Aux sources de l'imaginaire*, Dakar: IFAN Cheikh Anta Diop, 2009.

———, *Le Maraboutage au Sénégal*, Dakar: IFAN Cheikh Anta Diop, 2013.

Spencer, Nick, *Doing Good: A Future for Christianity in the 21st Century*, London: Theos, 2016.

———, *The Evolution of the West: How Christianity Has Shaped Our Values*, London: SPCK, 2016.

———, (ed.), *The Mighty and the Almighty: How Political Leaders Do God*, London: Biteback Publishing, 2017.

Spiro, Melford E., 'Religion: Problems of Definition and Explanation', in Michael Banton (ed.), *Anthropological Approaches to the Study of Religion*, London: Tavistock, 1966, 85–126.

Stark, Rodney, 'Efforts to Christianize Europe 400–2000', *JCR*, 16 (2001), 105–23.

————, *What Americans* Really *Believe*, Waco: Baylor University Press, 2008.

Stausberg, Michael (ed.), *Contemporary Theories of Religion: A Critical Companion*, Abingdon: Routledge, 2009.

Steinfels, Peter, *A People Adrift: The Crisis of the Roman Catholic Church in America*, New York: Simon and Schuster, 2003.

Stourton, James, *Kenneth Clark: Life, Art and Civilization*, London: Collins, 2016.

Sumption, Jonathan, *Pilgrimage: An Image of Mediaeval Religion*, London: Faber and Faber, 1975.

Taylor, Charles, *A Secular Age*, Cambridge, MA: Harvard University Press, 2007.

Thavis, John, *The Vatican Prophecies: Investigating Supernatural Signs, Apparitions, and Miracles in the Modern Age*, New York: Viking, 2015.

Thomas, Keith, *Religion and the Decline of Magic*, London: Penguin, 1973.

Tóibín, Colm, 'Putting Religion in Its Place', *LRB*, 23 October 2014, 19–23.

Tuchman, Barbara, *A Distant Mirror: The Calamitous 14th Century*, London: Macmillan, 1979 [1978].

UNICEF, *Children Accused of Witchcraft: An Anthropological Study of Contemporary Practices in Africa*, Dakar: UNICEF/WCARO, 2010.

Vinen, Richard, *National Service: A Generation in Uniform*, London: Penguin, 2015 [2014].

Voas, David, 'The Rise and Fall of Fuzzy Fidelity in Europe', *European Sociological Review*, 25, 2 (2009), 155–68.

————, and Steve Bruce, 'The 2001 Census and Christian Identification in Britain', *JCR*, 19 (2004), 23–8.

————, and Mark Chaves, 'Is the United Sates a Counterexample to the Secularization Thesis?', *American Journal of Sociology*, 121, 5 (2016), 1517–56.

Ward, Mrs Humphry, *Robert Elsmere*, Oxford: OUP, 1987 [1888].

Weinberg, Steven, 'Eye on the Present: The Whig History of Science', *NYRB*, 17 December 2015, 82–4.

————, *To Explain the World: The Discovery of Modern Science*, London: Penguin, 2016 [2015].

Wilson, Bryan, *Religion in Sociological Perspective*, Oxford: OUP, 1982.

Wolfe, Alan, 'Dieting for Jesus', *Prospect*, January 2004, 52–7.

————, 'The Opening of the Evangelical Mind', *Atlantic Monthly*, October 2000, 55–76.

————, *The Transformation of American Religion*, New York: Fourth Estate, 2003.

Wolff, Robert Lee, *Gains and Losses: Novels of Faith and Doubt in Victorian England*, New York: Garland Publishing, 1977.

Woodhead, Linda and Paul Heelas, *Religion in Modern Times*, Oxford: Blackwell, 2000.

SELECT BIBLIOGRAPHY

Woodward, Kenneth L., *Getting Religion: Faith, Culture and Politics from the Age of Eisenhower to the Era of Obama*, New York: Convergent, 2016.

Wootton, David, *The Invention of Science: A New History of the Scientific Revolution*, London: Allen Lane, 2015.

Wuthnow, Robert, *Inventing American Religion: Polls, Surveys, and the Tenuous Quest for a Nation's Faith*, New York: OUP, 2015.

Young, G.M., *Portrait of an Age*, London: Phoenix Press, 2002 [1936].

INDEX

Aaronovitch, David, 12–13
abortion, 57, 71, 72, 73
'Acres of Diamonds' sermon
  (Conwell), 78
African Americans, 72, 80, 86–7
African independent churches, ix
African Traditional Religion, 42–6
afterlife, 13, 23, 32, 66
AIDS (acquired immune deficiency
  syndrome), 42, 98
Albigensians, 32
albinism, 43–4
Alger, Horatio, 82
Allen, Asa Alonso, 79
Allen, John, 102–3
Altizer, Thomas Jonathan Jackson,
  58
American exceptionalism, 2, 68,
  69–91
American Religion, The (Bloom), 51
Anglicanism, Church of England,
  5, 8, 10, 21, 25, 56, 110
  and House of Lords, 102
  internal secularisation, 67–8
  and investment, 101
  Mrs Humphry Ward and, 55
  and social activism, 64
  and Trinity, 15

in Victorian period, 55, 56
Annan, Noel, 104–5
Anti-Modernist Oath (1910–67),
  60
Apologetics and Christian Doctrine
  (Sheehan), 64–5
Apologia (Newman), 55
Aquinas, Thomas, 32
Arianism, 20
Aristotle, 34
Arizona, United States, 80
Arnold, Matthew, 4, 26, 55
atheism, 7, 10, 11, 12, 52, 54, 90,
  96, 102, 106
Atonement, 31, 65
Augustine, Saint, 23, 40, 54
Aulen, Gustaf, 67
Austria, 7
Ayer, Alfred Jules, 41

Bacon, Francis, 34
Bakker, Jim and Tammy Faye, 79
Bakunin, Mikhail, 4
Balmer, Randall, 72
Bangui, Central African Republic,
  44
baptism, 30, 58
Baptists, 23, 70, 83, 84, 85

161

INDEX

INDEX

INDEX

INDEX

Euripides, 79
European Union, 20, 107
Evangelicalism, 2, 9, 16, 20,
   70–74, 83, 101, 110–11
Evangelium vitae, 73
Evolution of theWest, The (Spencer),
   52–3
Ex corde ecclesiae, 88

faculty club culture, 106
faith gospel, 13,79
Falwell, Jerry, 71
feminism, 60, 72, 86
Fernández-Armesto, Felipe, 108
festivals, 17
Feuerbach, Ludwig, 55
First Baptist Church, Dallas, 23
First Crusade (1095–1099), 30, 62
First Things, 74
FirstWorldWar (1914–18), 58
Flatt, Kevin, 110–11
Florida, United States, 80
football, 46, 48
Ford Foundation, 106
Ford, Gerald, 82
France, 5, 7
   Albigensians, 32
   Dreyfus Affair (1894–1906), 26
   mass attendance, 8
   Mitterrand, funeral of (1995), 48
   Revolution (1789–99), 26
   St Bartholomew's Day massacre
      (1572), 26
Francis, Pope, 65, 74, 75
Franck, Sebastian, 54
Fried, Johannes, 95–6
Fukuyama, Francis, 37, 95
Fulton, John, 8
fundamentalism, 70–71
Future Church, The (Allen), 102–3
Future for Christianity, A (Spencer),
   67–8

Galen, 34
Galilei, Galileo, 34
gambling, 57
Garrigou-Lagrange, Réginald
   Marie, 59
Gellner, Ernest, 26, 36, 37, 39, 40
General Electric, 100–101
Georgetown University, 86, 88, 89
Gleason, Philip, 88
Glendenning,Tony, 57
globalisation, 96
gnosticism, 51
Gospel of Christian Atheism, The
   (Altizer), 58
Grace Baptist Church,
   Philadelphia, 78
Graham,William 'Billy', 71
Grammar of Assent (Newman), 56
Grayling, Anthony Clifford, 7
great ditch, 95, 111–12
Great Expectations (Dickens), 41
Gregory, Brad, 37, 38
gris-gris, 45, 46
Guéranger, Dom Prosper, 59
Guide for Pilgrims to Santiago, 18

Hadaway, C. Kirk, 15
Hagee, John, 13
Hagin, Kenneth, 79
Halliday, Fred, 93–4
Hanson, Mark, 67
Hare, David, 64
*Hartford Appeal for Theological
   Affirmation*, 91
Heelas, Paul, 4, 49
Hegel, GeorgWilhelm Friedrich,
   55
Helena, Saint, 62
Herberg,William, 4, 76
Heritage USA, 79
Hervieu-Léger, Danièle, 4

INDEX

INDEX

INDEX

Exporting Countries (OPEC), 78

orphism, 51

Orthodox Christianity, 31–2, 54, 56, 61

Osteen, Joel, 80, 81

Our Age (Annan), 104–5

Outrageous Idea of Christian Scholarship, The (Marsden), 86–7

Oxfam, 103

Oxford University, 105

Pannenberg, Wolfhart, 67

papacy, 52, *see also* Pius XII, John XXIII, John Paul II, Benedict XVI, Francis

Papal States (754–1870), 7, 26

paradigms, 27

Parris, Matthew, 11

Paul, Saint, 51

Paul VI, Pope, 62, 74

Peale, Norman Vincent, 78–9

Peel, John, 1, 5, 9, 11, 94

Pelagianism, 30

Pell, George, 104

Pentecostalism, 79, 103

Perfect, Simon, 90

Pew Research Center, 5, 12

Philadelphia, Pennsylvania, 78

Phillips, Howard, 72

Phoenix, Arizona, 80

Piepkorn, Arthur Carl, 67

pilgrimage, 18, 24, 30

Pinomaa, Lennart, 67

Pius XII, Pope, 59

Plague of Justinian (541–2), 33

Plato, 27

Plutarch, 34

Poland, 19, 26, 75

Political Order in Changing Societies (Huntington), 100

polling, 15–7

Polo, Marco, 96

Poor Richard's Almanac, 82

Populorum progressio, 74

Portrait of an Age (Young), 56

Posner, Sarah, 72

Powell, Colin, 82

Power of Positive Thinking, The (Peale), 78–9

Presbyterianism, 23, 78, 83

Preus, Robert, 67

prosperity gospel, 2, 24, 77–83

Protestantism, 5, 60, 94, 103

evangelical, 24

in Global South, 24

liberal theology, 58

and modernity, 36

in Northern Ireland, 6, 7, 8

Reformation (1517–1648), 5, 27, 62, 103, 112

World Council of Churches, 15, 60–61

PTL Club, 79

Ptolemy, 34

Purgatory, 30, 31, 65

Puritanism, 36, 37

Putin, Vladimir, 20

Putnam, Robert, 47–8, 82

Quanbeck, Warren, 67

Quebec, 9

racism, 16, 72

Rahner, Karl, 66

Reagan, Ronald, 10, 82

reason, 2, 8, 37, 42, 52, 99–100, 109

reconciliation, 63

Reformation (1517–1648), 5, 27, 62, 103, 112

reiki, 49

reincarnation, 18

relics, 28, 62

169